Behind the Red Curtain

THE AZRIELI SERIES OF HOLOCAUST SURVIVOR MEMOIRS:
PUBLISHED TITLES

ENGLISH TITLES

Across the Rivers of Memory by Felicia Carmelly
Album of My Life by Ann Szedlecki
Alone in the Storm by Leslie Vertes
As the Lilacs Bloomed by Anna Molnár Hegedűs
Bits and Pieces by Henia Reinhartz
A Drastic Turn of Destiny by Fred Mann
E/96: Fate Undecided by Paul-Henri Rips
Fleeing from the Hunter by Marian Domanski
From Generation to Generation by Agnes Tomasov
Gatehouse to Hell by Felix Opatowski
Getting Out Alive by Tommy Dick
The Hidden Package by Claire Baum
Hope's Reprise by David Newman
If, By Miracle by Michael Kutz
If Home Is Not Here by Max Bornstein
If Only It Were Fiction by Elsa Thon
In Fragile Moments by Zsuzsanna Fischer Spiro/ *The Last Time* by Eva Shainblum
In Hiding by Marguerite Élias Quddus
Inside the Walls by Eddie Klein
Joy Runs Deeper by Bronia and Joseph Beker
Knocking on Every Door by Anka Voticky
Little Girl Lost by Betty Rich
Memories from the Abyss by William Tannenzapf/ *But I Had a Happy Childhood*
   by Renate Krakauer
My Heart Is At Ease by Gerta Solan
A Name Unbroken by Michael Mason
Never Far Apart by Kitty Salsberg and Ellen Foster
The Shadows Behind Me by Willie Sterner
Spring's End by John Freund
Stronger Together by Ibolya Grossman and Andy Réti
Suddenly the Shadow Fell by Leslie Meisels with Eva Meisels
Survival Kit by Zuzana Sermer
Tenuous Threads by Judy Abrams/ *One of the Lucky Ones* by Eva Felsenburg Marx
Traces of What Was by Steve Rotschild
Under the Yellow and Red Stars by Alex Levin
Vanished Boyhood by George Stern
The Violin by Rachel Shtibel/ *A Child's Testimony* by Adam Shtibel
W Hour by Arthur Ney
We Sang in Hushed Voices by Helena Jockel
The Weight of Freedom by Nate Leipciger
Where Courage Lives by Muguette Myers

TITRES FRANÇAIS

L'Album de ma vie par Ann Szedlecki
L'Antichambre de l'enfer par Felix Opatowski
Cachée par Marguerite Élias Quddus
Citoyen de nulle part par Max Bornstein
Étoile jaune, étoile rouge par Alex Levin
La Fin du printemps par John Freund
Fragments de ma vie par Henia Reinhartz
Frapper à toutes les portes par Anka Voticky
De génération en génération par Agnes Tomasov
L'Heure W par Arthur Ney
Une jeunesse perdue par George Stern
Les lieux du courage par Muguette Myers
Matricule E/96 par Paul-Henri Rips
Nous chantions en sourdine par Helena Jockel
Objectif : survivre par Tommy Dick
Les Ombres du passé par Willie Sterner
Que Renaisse Demain par Elsa Thon
Retenue par un fil par Judy Abrams/ *Une question de chance*
    par Eva Felsenburg Marx
Seule au monde par Betty Rich
Si, par miracle par Michael Kutz
Soudain, les ténèbres par Leslie Meisels
Souvenirs de l'abîme par William Tannenzapf / *Le Bonheur de l'innocence*
    par Renate Krakauer
Un terrible revers de fortune par Fred Mann
Traqué par Marian Domanski
Trousse de survie par Zuzana Sermer
Le Violon par Rachel Shtibel/ *Témoignage d'un enfant* par Adam Shtibel

Behind the Red Curtain: My Mother's Two Victories

Maya Rakitova

THE AZRIELI FOUNDATION
www.azrielifoundation.org

Cover and book design by Mark Goldstein
Endpaper maps by Martin Gilbert
Map on page xxv by François Blanc

LIBRARY AND ARCHIVES CANADA CATALOGUING IN PUBLICATION

Rakitova, Maya, 1931–, author
   Behind the red curtain: my mother's two victories/ Maya Rakitova.

(Azrieli series of Holocaust survivor memoirs. Series VIII)
Includes index.
ISBN 978-1-988065-13-7 (paperback)

1. Rakitova, Maya, 1931–. 2. Holocaust, Jewish (1939–1945) – Ukraine – Transnistria (Territory under German and Romanian occupation, 1941–1944) – Personal narratives. 3. Jewish children in the Holocaust – Ukraine – Transnistria (Territory under German and Romanian occupation, 1941–1944) – Biography. 4. Transnistria (Ukraine : Territory under German and Romanian occupation, 1941–1944) – Biography. I. Azrieli Foundation, issuing body II. Title. III. Series: Azrieli series of Holocaust survivor memoirs. Series VI

DS135.U43R35 2016   940.53'18092   C2016-905839-5

The Azrieli Series of Holocaust Survivor Memoirs

Naomi Azrieli, Publisher

Jody Spiegel, Program Director
Arielle Berger, Managing Editor
Farla Klaiman, Editor
Matt Carrington, Editor
Elizabeth Lasserre, Senior Editor, French-Language Editions
Elin Beaumont, Senior Educational Outreach and Events Coordinator
Catherine Person, Educational Outreach and Events Coordinator,
    Quebec and French Canada
Marc-Olivier Cloutier, Educational Outreach and Events Assistant,
    Quebec and French Canada
Tim MacKay, Digital Platform Manager
Elizabeth Banks, Digital Asset Curator and Archivist
Susan Roitman, Office Manager (Toronto)
Mary Mellas, Executive Assistant and Human Resources (Montreal)

Mark Goldstein, Art Director
François Blanc, Cartographer
Bruno Paradis, Layout, French-Language Editions

Contents

Series Preface   xi
About the Glossary   xiii
Introduction *by Karel C. Berkhoff*   xv
Acknowledgements   xvii

Map   xxv
Dedication   xxvii
Author's Preface   xxix

Revolutionary Beginnings   1
A Man of Principle   9
On the Move   15
Desperate Efforts   25
Hiding in the Open   37
Return to Life   43
Epilogue   47

"Comrade Rakitov": A Poem by Valentin Berestov   55

Glossary   57
Photographs   67
Index   77

Series Preface:
In their own words. . .

In telling these stories, the writers have liberated themselves. For so many years we did not speak about it, even when we became free people living in a free society. Now, when at last we are writing about what happened to us in this dark period of history, knowing that our stories will be read and live on, it is possible for us to feel truly free. These unique historical documents put a face on what was lost, and allow readers to grasp the enormity of what happened to six million Jews – one story at a time.

David J. Azrieli, C.M., C.Q., M.Arch
Holocaust survivor and founder, The Azrieli Foundation

Since the end of World War II, over 30,000 Jewish Holocaust survivors have immigrated to Canada. Who they are, where they came from, what they experienced and how they built new lives for themselves and their families are important parts of our Canadian heritage. The Azrieli Foundation's Holocaust Survivor Memoirs Program was established to preserve and share the memoirs written by those who survived the twentieth-century Nazi genocide of the Jews of Europe and later made their way to Canada. The program is guided by the conviction that each survivor of the Holocaust has a remarkable story to tell, and that such stories play an important role in education about tolerance and diversity.

Millions of individual stories are lost to us forever. By preserving the stories written by survivors and making them widely available to a broad audience, the Azrieli Foundation's Holocaust Survivor Memoirs Program seeks to sustain the memory of all those who perished at the hands of hatred, abetted by indifference and apathy. The personal accounts of those who survived against all odds are as different as the people who wrote them, but all demonstrate the courage, strength, wit and luck that it took to prevail and survive in such terrible adversity. The memoirs are also moving tributes to people – strangers and friends – who risked their lives to help others, and who, through acts of kindness and decency in the darkest of moments, frequently helped the persecuted maintain faith in humanity and courage to endure. These accounts offer inspiration to all, as does the survivors' desire to share their experiences so that new generations can learn from them.

The Holocaust Survivor Memoirs Program collects, archives and publishes these distinctive records and the print editions are available free of charge to educational institutions and Holocaust-education programs across Canada. They are also available for sale to the general public at bookstores. All revenues to the Azrieli Foundation from the sales of the Azrieli Series of Holocaust Survivor Memoirs go toward the publishing and educational work of the memoirs program.

~

The Azrieli Foundation would like to express appreciation to the following people for their invaluable efforts in producing this book: Doris Bergen, Sherry Dodson (Maracle Inc), Barbara Kamieński, Therese Parent, and Margie Wolfe & Emma Rodgers of Second Story Press.

About the Glossary

The following memoir contains a number of terms, concepts and historical references that may be unfamiliar to the reader. For information on major organizations; significant historical events and people; geographical locations; religious and cultural terms; and foreign-language words and expressions that will help give context and background to the events described in the text, please see the glossary beginning on page 57.

Introduction

Maya Rakitova's book is a breathtaking tale of lives destroyed, or all but destroyed, by the criminal political regimes of Stalin and Hitler. It tells the story of her life and that of her closest relatives in various corners of the Soviet Union, and of her two emigrations – to Poland shortly after Stalin's death in 1953 and to Canada in 1981. Timothy Snyder's 2010 bestseller *Bloodlands: Europe Between Hitler and Stalin* raised public awareness of the pre-war and wartime history of the regions "between Germany and Russia," where Rakitova's book is set, to an unusually high level. Nevertheless, the number of auto-biographical texts in English about those lands remains small. That alone makes this memoir very welcome.

Rakitova had formulated some of her recollections earlier, in 1997, when she agreed to be videotaped about the Holocaust by the Shoah Visual History Foundation, established by filmmaker Steven Spielberg. For this book, she used not only her own recollections but also those of her elder brother and her mother's brother. The Russian version of her text appeared in the Kiev journal *Holocaust and Modernity* in 2009, under the title "The Two Victories of My Mother." That same year, Yad Vashem in Israel decided to award the title of Righteous Among the Nations to her Ukrainian rescuer, Anna (Anastasia) Mikheyeva (1904–1978).

Rakitova's parents were Jewish. Her mother, we learn, was from

the Ukrainian city of Vinnitsa/Vinnytsia, while her father came from
Brichany/Briceni, a Bessarabian city today in northern Moldova.
Rakitova herself was born in Smolensk in the Russian Soviet Federal Socialist Republic, on June 4, 1931. It was a very turbulent time
throughout the world, and thus for the Jewish citizens of the Soviet
Union as well. This community had been and still was experiencing
rapid changes. Officially, according to Bolshevik Communist ideology, Jews did not merit any protection as a national minority because
they lacked their own territory. They were supposed to assimilate.
In practice, however, Soviet policy varied. On the positive side, Jews
benefited from the Soviet ban on antisemitic discrimination. A criminal code prescribed up to two years of detention for "incitement of
national or religious hatred or discord," which made citizens think
twice before, for instance, slurring Jews as *zhidy*, or kikes. A growing
body of research suggests that the Soviet policy shaped public per-
ceptions and conduct.

Jews were therefore able to advance in many professions and positions hitherto closed to them. By the early 1920s, they made up 13.6
per cent of all Communist Party members in Ukraine. (Over half were
Russian and close to a quarter were Ukrainian.) This was well above
the proportion of Jews in Soviet Ukraine's population. Jews even as-
sumed prominent roles in the Soviet political police (first Cheka,
then GPU, then NKVD), although never to the point that they domi-
nated it – contrary to the stereotype of "Jewish Bolshevism" wildly
popular within and, above all, outside the Soviet Union. A Jewish cultural environment developed that was secular and anti-religious but
offered numerous Yiddish theatres, journals, newspapers, and works
of Yiddish poetry and prose.

During the 1930s, however, as Stalin amassed ever more power,
the presence of Jews within the Party and among the political police
began to decline again. Jewish activists were persecuted, alongside
other intellectuals in Soviet Ukraine. The decade also saw accelera-
tion of the longer shift among Soviet Jews toward the Russian lan-

guage. At the beginning of the twentieth century, Yiddish had been the mother tongue of almost all of Ukraine's Jews, but after the revolutions of 1917 the language steadily lost ground: Jews increasingly started using Russian, the language of the cities and of the Soviet Union's largest recognized national group. By 1941, it was rare to find Jewish adults or children who used Yiddish as their first language.

Rakitova's father, Grigory, initially was typical of many Jewish males born in the late nineteenth century and active in the Soviet Union during the 1920s and 1930s. Having survived an anti-Jewish pogrom in Kishinev/Chişinău before the revolution, he became convinced that radical changes were needed. An outward sign of his conviction was that he changed his last name from Rabinovich to Rakitov. With his non-Jewish-sounding name, he supported the revolution of February 1917 and the Bolshevik takeover in November 1917. He probably felt that his choice for the Bolshevik cause was justified when civil war broke out and tens of thousands of Jews were killed in pogroms. Some 40 per cent of the pogroms in Ukraine were perpetrated by Ukrainian troops ostensibly loyal to a new Ukrainian government led by Symon Petliura.

Grigory helped consolidate the victorious side, the Bolshevik regime, which called itself Soviet. His work in government in various places (Vinnitsa, Poltava, Kaluga and Smolensk) offered his family a comparatively high living standard and contacts with prominent leaders, such as the commander of the Belorussian Military District, Yeronim Uborevich, and Yona Yakir and Lev Kamenev, both of Jewish descent. But Rakitova believes that her father felt guilty: the revolution had not given the positive results he had been expecting.

Two years before Rakitova was born, her parents and brother moved to Smolensk, where her father took up a position in the Communist Party committee for the newly created Western Oblast (province). Four years later, in 1933, Rakitov became chair of the *oblast* administration. Much of the paper trail of his work was found in the Smolensk Archive, captured by the German invaders in 1941 and taken by American forces to the United States after the war. This archive offered scholars starved for inside information a striking insight into the working of the Stalinist system. Rakitova's father appeared in the key publication based on these documents, Merle Fainsod's 1958 monograph *Smolensk under Soviet Rule*.

Like so many of his associates, Grigory was arrested by the NKVD in Stalin's Great Terror of the late 1930s, accused of membership in a terrorist anti-Soviet organization and executed. As was typical of Soviet practice, his wife did not know that she had become a widow for a long time. After several years of stonewalling, she was told that her husband was serving a prison sentence without right to correspondence. Only in 1956 did she and her children hear he had died – supposedly in 1940 and not because of any death sentence. Only in 1988 did the full truth emerge.

By Soviet law, the other Rakitovs – Maya, her mother and her brother – should have been arrested as "family members of traitors to the Motherland." However, as a favour from the deputy leader of the NKVD, Latvian-born Leonid Zakovsky, known as the "butcher of Leningrad," the law was not applied to them. As Rakitova writes, they had no idea about this for decades.

The three fled to Ukraine, often alternating between Vinnitsa, located in the historic region of Podolia, about two hundred kilometres southwest of Kiev, and Odessa. Vinnitsa and Odessa were both targeted in the Great Terror, but it somehow bypassed the Rakitovs. Maya likely had no clue about all of this at the time. Still, it is surprising that she writes nothing about the infamous NKVD mass graves in Vinnitsa, which the Nazis excavated in 1943 and declared to be the killing site for "ten thousand Ukrainians."

Rakitova then tells her astonishing story from the midst of Ukraine's Holocaust – in the German-ruled Reichskommissariat Ukraine (directed by Reichskommissar Erich Koch) and then in Romanian-ruled Transnistria. About 60 per cent of Ukraine's pre-war Jewish population was murdered in the Holocaust in less than two years. In the middle of 1941, there were about 2.7 million Jews in the territory of what today is the independent state of Ukraine (including the Crimean peninsula). Approximately 900,000 fled or were evacuated from Ukraine to the east in time. But some 1.5 million of Ukraine's Jews died at the hands of Germans, Romanians, Hungarians, Ukrainians, and others. The Jewish communities of the western regions of Galicia, Volhynia and Podolia, with cities such as Lviv/Lwów/Lvov, Rivne/Równe/Rovno and also Vinnitsa, were almost entirely destroyed.

The Holocaust in Vinnitsa is known in the West above all from a sickening photograph often called "The Last Jew," most likely taken near that city. (The United States Holocaust Memorial Museum shows it online in its Photo Archives as Photograph #64407.) German soldiers of the Waffen-SS and the Reich Labour Service look on as a member of one of the notorious mobile killing squads, the Einsatzgruppen, points his extended arm at a Jewish man kneeling on the edge of a mass grave already filled with corpses. He holds a pistol and is about to shoot. The victim seems to look into the camera. When this shooting occurred is unclear, but 1941 seems likely. The photograph is often reproduced, sometimes even – in my view, unethically – on the cover of books.

It does, however, represent the "other" Holocaust, one that did not involve death in camps but rather death by shooting. When wartime Ukraine is compared to other European regions, what stands out is that the vast majority of Ukraine's Jews were murdered in mass shootings close to home, and within days, weeks or at most months after the Germans arrived. The latter point – the haste with which Ukraine's Jews were murdered, be it by Germans, Romanians or others – is one of the Holocaust's most perplexing aspects. The historian Alexander Kruglov has estimated that in 1941 alone, Ukraine's average daily Jewish death toll was more than 2,600, while in 1942 it was still more than 2,000. Other historians believe the daily average in 1942 was even higher than in 1941.

In all, there were some two thousand German murder actions in Ukraine, actions that took the form of shootings of large and small groups of Jews. Soon after the German invasion that began in late June 1941, ever greater proportions of Jews were murdered in a progression that included able-bodied men (early July), Jews among the prisoners of war (middle of July), and women and children (late August).

This also happened in Vinnitsa, where some 33,000 inhabitants, over a third of the population, were Jewish. Yiddish culture had only recently come under sustained attack there; well into the 1930s, the city had a theatre, choir, newspaper, court chamber and even a police station that all functioned in Yiddish.

There were rumours about Nazi Germany, but often those were disbelieved. Still, when the Germans invaded, half of the city's Jews had been able to leave ahead of them. The city was occupied on July 19, 1941. The occupiers appointed a Jewish council, forced all Jews to wear armbands with the Star of David, placed them under guard in several locations, and ordered the non-Jewish population to immediately sever all contacts with them. The first major shooting action against the 15,000 Jews remaining in Vinnitsa took place within weeks.

Most of the city's Jews were killed in two large-scale murder operations in September 1941 and April 1942. These were perpetrated, in particular, by Einsatzkommando 6 (part of Einsatzgruppe C), and by German Reserve Police Battalion 45. The latter battalion murdered more than 10,000 Jewish men, women and children on a single day – September 19, 1941. About a thousand skilled workers were temporarily spared and used for various works, including the construction of Hitler's nearby "Werewolf" headquarters. Research on this element of the Holocaust has progressed thanks to Ukrainian citizens such as local archivist Faina Vinokurova and Alexander Kruglov.

Fortunately, Rakitova evaded these mass shootings, and in the spring of 1942, she managed to arrive in Transnistria, an entity (under Governor Gheorghe Alexianu) that was only formally separate from the Romanian state. Comprising territory in today's Ukraine and Moldova, Transnistria had about two hundred ghettos, concentration camps and penal labour camps. In the most lethal of these camps, Romanian, Ukrainian and ethnic German policemen carried out mass shootings of Jews.

Transnistria was a horrible place, but survival was less difficult than in German-ruled Ukraine, particularly late in the war. That was because the Romanian leadership had made a turnaround. At first, State Leader Ion Antonescu ordered that the Jews in recovered Romanian territory (Bessarabia and Bukovina) be condemned to death. But then, in the fall of 1942, he changed his mind, mainly in view of the course of the war, and by April 1943, he no longer let Jews be deported to Nazi death camps.

Rakitova was mostly in the capital of Transnistria, Odessa, and survived there under the name Maria, after a baptism at age eleven. (The Orthodox priest had to lift her up for the prescribed rite and had some difficulty with it.) Had the girl arrived in Odessa earlier, it is unlikely that she would have survived. On October 22, 1941, a Soviet mine in the Romanian army headquarters in the city killed a general and sixty officers and soldiers. As in Kiev (site of the notorious Babi Yar massacre of September 29–30, 1941), the occupiers blamed the Jews and quickly killed them in revenge. Of about 90,000 Jews present in Odessa at that time, including many refugees, approximately 25,000 were murdered in just two days. In November 1941, the Jews were ordered to move to a ghetto in the Slobodka city district. In January 1942, they were deported from the city altogether, to perform forced labour further north and east. It was a massive exodus in which at least one in four deportees died on the way. That Rakitova arrived after all of this helps explain why she considered the Romanians less zealously antisemitic.

She describes how during the summer of 1943, she saw in Odessa mysterious lodgers, young men said to be from Poland, some of

whom wore German military uniforms. The woman who was res-
cuing her, Anna Mikheyeva, suspected that one of them was Jewish,
Rakitova writes. But it is actually likely that all were. Other memoirs
tell us that Jews from occupied Poland organized an escape route to
the east, with the ultimate goal of ending up in central Romania. Pre-
tending to be non-Jewish Poles, they took up jobs at construction
sites, sometimes as far east as Kiev or Dnipro/Dnepropetrovsk, and
sometimes they took Jewish women there, too. Some of these Jews
survived and later described their experiences. They include Amnon
Ajzensztadt, Jacob Gerstenfeld-Maltiel and Marian Pretzel.

How disgraceful that Rakitova's rescuer, Mikheyeva, was arrested
by the Soviet authorities and sentenced, in August 1945, to six years of
labour camp and confiscation of property. What initiated it remains
unclear, but she was accused of many things, including deliberately
not evacuating east in 1941 and praising the Romanian occupation.
She spent time in a Gulag camp in Estonia, moved back to Ukraine
(though not to Odessa) and obtained an official "rehabilitation" in
1961. This story was uncovered when, in 2003, Rakitova asked the
World-Wide Club of Odessites for help in finding information on
her rescuer. Six years later, archival researcher Igor Komarovsky re-
sponded and was able to provide the post-war details of Mikheyeva's life, documentation that helped Rakitova have her recognized as
Righteous Among the Nations.

Rakitova says herself that life in the Soviet Union "initially was
full of hopes," but that these were to turn into "numerous tragedies":
"Stalin's regime was one of the most terrible and meaningless in history. Young people who thought they were creating a world of justice
fell victim to unprecedented terror." For years, she lived in fear that
her father's arrest would become known, for then she would be dis-
criminated against. After Stalin died, it still remained impossible to
talk openly about either Stalin or the Nazis. And yet Rakitova seems
to be neutral about the post-Stalin Soviet political system. She would
have every right to be angry, but her memoir is not.

The cursory way in which the Germans appear in Rakitova's memoir is also remarkable. These invaders methodically killed all Jews, but this survivor prefers not to spend time commenting on these perpetrators. Not even the word "fascist" – the standard, though inaccurate, Soviet and post-Soviet term for the Nazis – appears. Ukrainian policemen are not condemned, and neither does Rakitova – in great contrast to most memoirs by Jewish survivors from western Ukraine's former Polish regions, Galicia and Volhynia – have harsh words for the Ukrainians (or other non-Jews) as a people. One likely reason is that against all odds, which included, as Rakitova herself and many others called it, "typically Jewish" features, Rakitova survived thanks to Ukrainian rescuers.

At least as important in explaining Rakitova's perspective, however, may be her own unwillingness, for many years, to talk about her past. She considered the awful memories an obstacle to a normal life and had tried to forget her childhood. That she testified all the same is reason to be grateful.

Karel C. Berkhoff
NIOD Institute for War, Holocaust and Genocide Studies, Amsterdam
2016

FURTHER READING

Karel C. Berkhoff, *Harvest of Despair: Life and Death in Ukraine under Nazi Rule* (Cambridge, Massachusetts: The Belknap Press of Harvard University Press, 2004).
Karel C. Berkhoff, "The Holocaust in Ukraine," EHRI Online Course in Holocaust Studies, http://training.ehri-project.eu/unit/3-holocaust-ukraine (2015; last accessed August 24, 2016).
Diana Dumitru, *The State, Antisemitism, and Collaboration in the Holocaust: The Borderlands of Romania and the Soviet Union* (Cambridge: Cambridge University Press, 2016).

Igor Komarovsky, "Account of a Life Story Fact-Finding," at http://www.odessit-club.org/reading_room/komarovsky/mikheeva_angl.php (last accessed August 24, 2016).

Yad Vashem, "The Untold Stories: The Murder Sites of the Jews in the Occupied Territories of the Former USSR," http://www.yadvashem.org/untoldstories/index.html (last accessed August 24, 2016).

LEGEND

Pre-War Borders

War-Time Borders

0   200   400km

N

© 2016 - The Azrieli Foundation

The most interesting times for historians are generally the most difficult for the people who have the misfortune to live in them. My story is dedicated to my family members, who lived in such times; my mother, who survived every cruel ordeal; and her friends, who risked their lives for our sake. I must also pay tribute to my brother, Leonid, who told me about my mother's younger years – my mother had never talked to me about them, perhaps because I never asked her, something I regret to this day. Leonid was also the one who told me about our father, whom I hardly remembered. Leonid was nine years older than me, admired our father and revered his memory. Shortly before Leonid's death in Israel on February 11, 2002, I asked him to tell me about our father, and it is his reminiscences on which the beginning of my story is based.

I would also like to thank Victor Krupnik, not only for translating my memoir from Russian but also for his valuable advice and explanatory additions for English-speaking readers.

Author's Preface

The idea of writing a memoir of my childhood came to mind several years ago, and since everyone's childhood is ultimately associated with one's mother, this story was written to honour my mother. Nowadays the shelves of our bookstores are full of memoirs of well-known people. My mother was not famous, yet she was not an ordinary person. A very hard fate befell her, but she lived her life without ever losing her courage. Facing certain death, she managed to save herself and her children twice – the first time from Stalin's prison camps and the second time from execution during the Nazi occupation of Ukraine. I think she was able to do this because of her extreme energy and uncommon courage, as well as her rare gift of attracting people.

One may ask why I decided to put pen to paper after so many years have passed. There are many reasons for this. My story presents further evidence of the way of life in the former USSR, a life that was initially full of hopes but that, ultimately, turned into numerous tragedies. Stalin's regime was one of the most terrible and meaningless in history. Young people who thought they were creating a world of justice fell victim to unprecedented terror. Then, in 1939, the war began, followed two years later by the Nazi occupation. Most people now know what this meant for the Jews, though some still do not want to believe it.

All my life I kept trying not to remember my childhood. Growing up, I lived through such hard times that any recollection of them would have prevented me from living a normal life, studying and working. I suppose that I have tried subconsciously to forget those years, and that is why some details left in my memory are hazy – I don't remember the exact sequence of events, except for the turning points and critical moments when I was seized with fear. I recollect those moments like separated frames of an old, half-forgotten movie.

Decades after the war, I hosted a Russian-language program broadcast on Radio Canada International, and I received a lot of letters from my listeners. Once I opened one sent from Vinnitsa, my childhood town, and I suddenly burst into tears. My colleague, who was sitting next to me, asked compassionately, "What happened, Maya?" As I looked at the postcard with a view of my native town, I recognized the exact place where I had been standing late at night, sixty years earlier, sobbing violently in fear and despair because I had nowhere to go. A few days before, the Germans had seized all the members of my family and executed them in a forest near Vinnitsa. Only my mother had managed to escape, but I didn't know where she was. All day long I had been searching throughout the town for her among her friends and acquaintances, but I hadn't found her. It was getting dark and I did not know where else to go. These are the kinds of moments that stand out in my memory.

Though I hardly think back to those days and events, as people get older their memories often return to their pasts. I cannot explain why it happens; probably we have more time to think about our lives, to answer questions as to why we lived them one way and not another, to remember all the mistakes we made and how they affected the lives of our loved ones. Furthermore, there is a strong desire to tell our children and grandchildren about their ancestors; in part, this is what I seek.

Revolutionary Beginnings

Vinnitsa, which was part of the Russian Empire until 1917, is located on a bend of the Southern Bug River, and its Old Town sits on the opposite bank. This is where my mother, Zinaida Brik, was born. She was the third of ten children in a Jewish family of modest means. Before the Bolshevik revolution in 1917, her father, Moisie, or Moshe, Brik, had a trade business, which was typical for the majority of Jews at that time. After the revolution, the new authorities forced him to get rid of his business. My grandfather devoted himself instead to gardening, in spite of the fact that this was unusual for Jewish men. He turned out to have a calling for it, and his garden was famous among the citizens of the Old Town.

Vinnitsa is now part of Ukraine and its population in 2013 was about 370,000, but in the interwar years it was a relatively small town. Many Jews lived there and, not without reason, one of the town districts was named Yerusalimka, Small Jerusalem. During that pre-war time, I would see old, bearded Jewish men sitting on benches near their poor houses on the outskirts of Vinnitsa, discussing the problems of the world. I suppose they were already worried about the situation of the Jews in Germany.

My grandfather was born in Yerusalimka; after his marriage to my grandmother, Sima, he moved with his family to the Old Town, which looked like a village buried in the foliage of gardens. There were many small cob wall houses with thatched roofs, but my grandfather had a brick house, one of the best in town, with an iron roof and an enormous garden and orchard where he planted each tree with his own hands.

During the summer, my grandfather was in the orchard by dawn, dealing with the endless budding and grafting of trees growing a variety of different fruits. Never again in my life would I eat such aromatic, sweet and juicy fruit as the ones from my grandfather's orchard.

My mother had grown up in the Old Town, which was populated mainly by Ukrainians, and she socialized with the local youth. She wore clothes in the same style as the local country girls. My mother was a very sociable person, and I believe that if she had lived in a Jewish community, she would probably have felt a lack of freedom within its strict boundaries and would sooner or later have left it. Unlike her sisters and brothers, who had a university or at least a secondary school education, my mother had only four years of primary school. Sometimes, with a smile that showed the presence of some guilt, she would explain to me that she had had to help her father in his store and there was no time left for studies. My grandfather considered her the most capable and appropriate person for his business, and I tend to believe it, since my mother really possessed outstanding management abilities. She compensated for her lack of education with a passion for reading. My mother told me that in her early childhood, since her father would always find more important things for her to do, she would hide in the attic to read books. Her love of reading probably was the reason she could be on equal terms in discussions with highly educated people. She especially liked to discuss political matters, although her interest in politics no doubt came after the revolution, which had changed her life so dramatically.

My mother connected with the revolution through her desire to be with my father. In 1916, during World War I, soldiers were quartered in my grandfather's house because it was one of the best houses in the Old Town. My father-to-be, Grigory Rakitov, whose real name was Rabinovich, was among those soldiers. That was when he set eyes on my mother for the first time. In 1916, he was already a dedicated Bolshevik, but his roots were far from revolutionary.

My father was born on February 28, 1894, in the small town of Brichany, Bessarabia. Unlike my mother, my father was brought up in a religious family where Jewish traditions were strictly observed. He studied in a cheder, a religious Jewish school for boys, where he showed a lot of diligence and talent. At the age of twelve, he started giving private lessons to children from wealthy families. He kept doing this for a living even later, when he was a young man.

What made a youth who had received a religious Jewish upbringing become a revolutionist? In April 1903, when my father was nine, he and his father witnessed, and survived, the infamous anti-Jewish pogrom in Kishinev. That year began a wave of anti-Jewish pogroms through southern Russia that continued to 1906. I was told that in my father's native town of Brichany, a pogrom was also expected, but workers in the railway workshops at the local Oknitsy (now Ocniţa, Moldova) station took control of the situation, preventing violence from breaking out. It was probably then that, being a responsive and impressionable boy, my father decided to devote himself to the "social and economic liberation of workers."

In fact, many Jews played a role in the Russian social revolution. Deprived of civil rights, they hoped that the revolution would bring them equality. Now, in the twenty-first century, we know of all the terrifying consequences of the revolution, but at the beginning of the twentieth century many young people enthusiastically adopted the utopian ideas of revolution, envisaging the abolishment of human evil and the creation of a new world based on universal justice. In reality the revolution abolished human flaws and virtues together because in human nature, good and evil are never far from one another. Unfortunately, an understanding of this came too late. Many honest and remarkable people couldn't believe that all the ordeals caused by the revolution were the result of the terror created by Stalin.

In any case, in 1912 my father moved to Kishinev, where he attempted to continue his education and kept giving lessons in order to earn a living. In Kishinev he joined the Bund, the General Jewish Workers' Union in Lithuania, Poland and Russia, which represented the left wing of the political movement at that time. It was here that my father met Yona Yakir, a prominent figure in post-revolution Soviet Russia who would later become a Red Army commander. Their paths would cross again during the Bolshevik Revolution in 1917.

In 1913, at the age of nineteen, my father moved to Odessa. He tried to enter university, which was not easy because of an established quota for Jews. Though he had passed the high school examinations, he was not admitted, and he eventually enrolled as an external student. That year he also joined the Bolshevik Party, officially called the Russian Social Democratic Labour Party. When World War I began the following year, he went back to Brichany. He was not initially recruited to serve in the army because he had tuberculosis, which some other members of his family had also suffered from. However, in 1916 he was recruited and sent to Vinnitsa with an army formation. Shortly thereafter he joined the Military Revolutionary Committee and took part in a battle against military cadets of the Imperial Russian Army in October 1917. My father was one of the three leaders of the armed revolt in Vinnitsa, representing the army, while Nikolai Tarnogrodsky represented the factory workers and Alexei Snegov the university students. After the Bolsheviks came to power, my father became a member of the Regional Executive Committee. In 1918, shortly after the beginning of the Civil War, Vinnitsa was captured by the Ukrainian Army, led by *Ataman*, Supreme Commander, Symon Petliura, and my father went underground. The Communist Party Central Committee sent him to Odessa.

In 1918, the city of Odessa presented quite a mixed picture: in the streets one could meet Frenchmen, Greeks, Petliura's militants, officers and soldiers of the anti-Bolshevik White Army – and criminal elements of all kinds. This period of my father's life in Odessa was full of adventures. He was finally admitted to university and was a leader in an underground student political organization that my brother said was called Spartak. After the Red Army freed Odessa, he became a commissar, a political leader, at the university and got a position as treasurer on the City Council.

In June 1919, as the White Army approached Odessa again, a military formation, the 45th Rifle Division, was raised to defend the city. Natives of Bessarabia made up a large part of this division. Its commander was Yona Yakir, and my father initially was deputy chief of political matters but soon was named commissar. My father stayed with the division, which played an important role in the defence of the revolution and was mentioned in many historical and literary writings, until the end of the Civil War in 1921.

$\sim$

My father's official Soviet biography states that he remained in the position of commissar of the 45th Division until 1921. By that time, his tuberculosis had progressed, forcing him to leave the army. Even so, he never stopped his activities as a revolutionist. The Central Committee sent him to Vinnitsa to get rid of numerous bands that were terrorizing the locals, especially members of the Jewish community, who had become the main target of the bandits' non-stop raids. My father was accompanied by Leonid Zakovsky, who would later rise to a highly influential position. Both of them rented a room in my grandfather's house, where my mother lived. She was a joyful and smart girl who could dance and sing, and both men soon fell in love with her. Zakovsky was very attractive to women – he was handsome, easygoing and cheerful – but my mother gave her heart to my father.

As for Zakovsky, he stayed out of sight for a while. Thirteen years later, in December 1934, a popular Communist Party leader in Leningrad, Sergey Kirov, was assassinated, possibly by Stalin's order, and this marked the beginning of unprecedented mass terror. It was then that Zakovsky was appointed chief of the NKVD, the People's

Commissariat for Internal Affairs, in Leningrad. In this high post, he turned out to be a most cruel executioner.

Later on, when my brother asked my mother why she had chosen our father, she answered that he was a more positive and reliable man. Yet my mother's elder brother, Arkady, wrote the story of how my parents met in his memoir, giving quite a different description:

One day, soldiers of the local garrison were quartered in our house. One of the soldiers, a Jew, Grigory Rakitov, tried everything to deserve Zina's special attention. When the revolution began, Rakitov became thoroughly engrossed in it and soon found himself in the 45th Division. He took part in combat at different fronts in the Ukraine, often in Podolia, a region around Vinnitsa. One fine day Zina just left home with Rakitov to accompany him on his next military campaign.

In those days, Vinnitsa changed rulers many times. After the Red Army, the White Army would come, displaced in turn by Petliura's army, and so on. Sometimes people had breakfast under one government and went to bed under another. One currency was in use in the morning and another one at night – all the same good-for-nothing scraps of paper. When the 45th Division took up in Vinnitsa again, it was decided to celebrate Zina and Grigory's wedding. A modest celebration was held in the evening, attended by guests including commander Yona Yakir with his wife, chief of staff and other officers.

While he does not state exactly when this wedding took place, Uncle Arkady says quite clearly that my mother had followed my father before their marriage. Imagining the time and a conservative Jewish family's moral principles, one might conclude that such behaviour in a young girl would be regarded as very adventurous and thoughtless. My mother had never told me about this; moreover, I don't think that my uncle's story reflected the real events given the conservative nature of the time, but knowing my mother's nature and her future destiny, I am pretty sure that she just followed her heart.

My parents married in 1921. At first, my father worked in Vinnitsa, but they didn't stay there for long. My father soon got a position as first secretary of the Government Committee in Poltava, where my brother, Leonid, was born in August 1922. My parents lived in Poltava until 1926, when my father got another position as first secretary in Kaluga.

My brother assured me that he remembered this time quite well. He told me that our mother was joyful and was always laughing and singing. I believe that she could have been like this, as she was cheerful and jovial by nature. Having grown up in a Ukrainian village, she liked to sing, as everybody in her family did. She had a good voice, a contralto, soft and rather sonorous at the same time. I remember her singing at home and at parties; her best-known performance was a romance song, "Pair of Bays." My mother was not only social but also very energetic. The role of a housewife never attracted her. In Kaluga, as soon as Leonid got a little older, she started working.

A Man of Principle

In 1929 my father got a new assignment, this time in Smolensk. That year, a new administrative and territorial division was created in the USSR: local *guberniya*, governorates, were transformed into *oblasts*, regions. The Bryansk and Smolensk governorates, as well as parts of the Moscow, Kaluga, Pskov and Tver governorates, were combined into the Western Oblast, a vast territory spread over 163,400 square kilometres. My father was assigned to the position of second secretary of the *oblast* committee. My brother mentioned that my father was going to take the position of first secretary, but Stalin objected and ordered that Ivan Rumyantsev be assigned instead, based on the fact that Rumyantsev had joined the Bolshevik Party nine years earlier than my father. But in my brother's opinion, Stalin could not forgive our father for a political mistake: once in Kaluga, he had sheltered Lev Kamenev and his family; Kamenev had been banned by the official regime because, while a member of the first Politburo, he had opposed Stalin. So Rumyantsev took the highest rank in the Western Oblast; the second position, according to the Soviet hierarchy, was chairman of the Executive Committee, which was taken by Ilya Shelekhes; and my father got the third position.

Leonid characterized Rumyantsev and his family as quite intelligent, modest and decent. As for Shelekhes, he came from an interesting Jewish family. Before the revolution, Shelekhes and his two brothers had been in the diamond business. After the revolution, one of the three brothers was charged with the theft of diamonds and executed, and the other two joined the Bolsheviks.

According to Leonid, those years in Smolensk were the happiest for him and for our parents. Nowadays, I suppose that nobody could have really been happy at that time; many people had a presentiment that Stalin's regime could bring nothing but misfortune. Leonid often stressed how different our parents were. To my great regret, I don't remember my father well, in part because he did not spend much time at home. That is why everything I know about my father I've learned from my brother, who worshipped him.

Our father was always scrupulous and ascetic. He never allowed himself or his family to take advantage of his high-ranking position. All his life was devoted to work and there was no time for the family. It is hard to blame him – to understand him you had to know the typical way of life at that time. Everybody in such positions worked until late and our father was no exception; he used to come home at 1:00 a.m. every morning. His time, his thoughts, his senses were fully consumed by the responsibilities he was charged with. And his thoughts, I suppose, were far from optimistic. I believe that he had long realized that the social system created in the Soviet Union by the Bolsheviks was quite far from the one he and his brothers-in-arms had been dreaming of in their youth.

The reality of everyday life didn't allow my father the slightest hint of luxury, if this word can be used in connection with the Soviet Union at the beginning of the 1930s. Though wartime had ended long before, he wore a soldier's blouse and a greatcoat. These I remembered the most – his greatcoat and his beard. He grew a beard back in 1919 as a commissar of the 45th Division, and there is a story behind it. In 1919, near Odessa, the White Army encircled two Red Army divisions, an encirclement so extensive that the soldiers had to fight through Imperial hordes for almost four hundred kilometres. Yan Gamarnik led the second division, and he and my father promised each other not to shave until they broke through the enemy's barriers. But, after the war ended, they decided to quit shaving and from then on left their beards untouched. Later, in 1930, Gamarnik rose to the leadership of the department of politics in the Red Army. He held this position until the ill-fated year of 1937, when his close army friends, the outstanding military leaders Marshals Mikhail Tukhachevsky and Yeronim Uborevich, were declared traitors and executed by Stalin's order. Gamarnik, having a premonition that he could be the next of Stalin's victims, committed suicide.

But to go back to my father, his decency was overwhelming; not only did he refuse any earthly blessings for himself, he was certain that his family's way of life must be the same. After our arrival in Smolensk, we lived in two rooms of a so-called communal apartment. Since the phenomenon of communal apartments belongs exclusively to Soviet Russia, it needs some explanation. One apartment was inhabited by several different families, one family to a room. All families shared in common one kitchen, one bathroom (if any) and one toilet. We were lucky to have two rooms; the family of a writer of children's books occupied another two rooms of the apartment. After one year or so, we moved to a three-room apartment in the same building that had suddenly become vacant. My nanny, Nyura, my brother, Leonid, and I shared the largest room. The smaller room was both our dining room and a study; my dad's bureau stood there, together with a couch and a bedside table with a portable gramophone on it. The third room, the smallest one, was my parents' bedroom.

In Smolensk, my mother had started working right away. In her early thirties, energetic and vigorous, with remarkable abilities, she managed the canteen that belonged to the Higher Party School. She quit her job not long before the day I was born in June 1931, but stayed home with me for just a month. Then a nanny was brought to our house, a fifteen-year-old country girl named Nyura. Being bright and diligent, she quickly learned about housekeeping from my mother and soon became a devoted friend of the whole family. She held an important place in my life and was strongly attached to me, and I reciprocated her affection. When my mother was absent, I stayed calm, but when Nyura was not with me, I would start sobbing violently.

In 1935, when I was four years old, we moved into a large, comfortable mansion. I remember this six-room house and the garden where I used to play with my friends. My father had agreed to this move not only because of my mother's influence, but also because his colleagues at work had persuaded him that a person of his rank should live in more appropriate conditions. The mansion was initially occupied by General Semyon Timoshenko, who had left when he received an assignment in Moscow. The house was then intended for the Armed Forces commander of Belorussia, Yeronim Uborevich. He was alone in Smolensk, as his wife worked in Moscow and all his family lived there. Uborevich persuaded my father to move into the mansion and Uborevich moved into the smaller apartment that had been intended for us. Uborevich was an outstanding military leader who was born into a family of Lithuanian peasants. He started his career during World War I as a junior officer in the Imperial Russian Army after graduating from artillery school. In 1917, he joined the Red Army, and one year later he had the opportunity to display his military talents during the Civil War in Russia. Well–educated and an expert on military matters, Uborevich had mastered military science through studies in Germany.

I remember Uborevich very well, probably because he spent a lot of time with Leonid and me. On Sundays, my father and other high-ranking persons with families would go out of town and gather in a big cottage, a *dacha*, which was named Volnerovo. Uborevich would make me sit down next to him and would tell the waiter, "Please bring cooked potatoes in their jackets for me and Mayechka!" I preferred potatoes in their skins because I was used to this simple meal from my early childhood. Perhaps Uborevich kept ordering the same potatoes for himself because he just wanted to keep me company. I think Uborevich liked children and missed his wife and daughter. In

Volnerovo, Uborevich often had long conversations with my brother and once invited him to his place. For company, he lived with an older woman, who served him for many years as a housekeeper, and her disabled grandson. That evening he talked to my brother about artillery, and after a while, Uborevich began to invite him over more and more often. Leonid insisted that his conversations with Uborevich had a big influence on his life, and that as a result of these chats he became an artillerist.

Our father did not spend time with us because he was too busy and all his energy and attention were focused on thousands of other people he was taking care of. I assume he subconsciously felt guilty for the results of the revolution, which were far from those he had believed in. I found indirect proof of his sensitivity in the Smolensk Archive, which had been captured by the Nazis during World War II, then fell into American hands and was subsequently returned to Russia. I also later found in the McGill University library a few history books based on documents from the Smolensk Archive. Among them were statements and complaints against local authorities made by civilians. Many of the documents have my father's instructions on how to resolve such concerns.

As a cheerful and sociable person, my mother most likely did not share my father's ideas about neglecting one's personal well-being for the sake of humanity's happiness. My father's excessive modesty was often a reason for her temper. She was a realist, blaming my father for his careless attitude toward our family's prosperity. My mother would have liked to be well dressed, living in a good apartment and enjoying the benefits of life.

I remember many people – representatives of factories and plants – coming to our house. In keeping with Soviet rules, everybody brought presents to my father, but he never allowed a single one to stay in the house. All the presents had to be sent to foster homes, hospitals or other institutions right away. My brother described an incident in his memoir:

One fine Sunday, two men appeared carrying an enormous case with a handle. They were managers of a musical instrument factory, and our father had been patronizing the construction and start-up of the factory. So these men came in and announced that they wanted to show the first sample of their product. When the case was opened, I saw a beautiful accordion with an engraved metal plate that read "To Dear Grigory D. Rakitov." I liked this accordion very much but I was not sure if my father was going to accept it. Regardless of my expectations, my dad thanked the factory managers and took the present. After they left, I rushed to the instrument but my father stopped me and ordered his driver, "Take this toy and bring it to the orphanage immediately!" I burst into tears and my mother stood up for me, blaming my father with trying my patience for nothing.

So, our father was decent and strict with no exceptions for anybody. Although my brother almost always took our father's side, Leonid nevertheless considered our mother right in criticizing him for his behaviour with us.

In January 1937, the one-hundredth anniversary of the death of the great Russian poet Alexander Pushkin was commemorated with events held all over Soviet Russia. A masked ball was to take place in our school, so my friend and I, as well as two other girls from our class and our teacher, headed to the local theatre to borrow costumes. A lot of costumes were tied into big heavy bundles and all of us together were not strong enough to carry them. I decided to call my father's driver, Lopatov (who was, by the way, a manager of a garage), and asked him to help us. Lopatov didn't see any problem with this and came with a car right away. We loaded in the costumes and he drove us to the school. A few days later, my father came home after work late, as usual, entered my room and woke me up. He did not usually hit me, but this time he grabbed me by the collar and started to shake me, yelling at me, berating me for the call I had made. Nobody was allowed to call for the car – not I, nor our mother. We could go by car only with our father or under extraordinary circumstances.

On the Move

In the beginning of May 1937, my father was appointed chairman of the *oblast* committee in the town of Kursk. This assignment came unexpectedly, and while he moved to Kursk, more than five hundred kilometres away, my mother, my brother and I stayed in Smolensk. Our father phoned us from Kursk every day, often with scary news – there had been a series of arrests of political and military figures in both Kursk and Smolensk.

On June 18, Ivan Rumyantsev, the first secretary of the *oblast* committee in Smolensk, was arrested. Mother understood that the critical moment had come and rushed to Kursk to discuss with Father our moving to his place. She thought our father might soon be arrested, too, though he himself did not expect such a thing. My mother came back two days later and began to pack our belongings right away. Her elder sister, Sonya, came from Vinnitsa to help us. My brother and all the people in our neighbourhood thought we were going to leave for Kursk. On July 2, Mother sent Father a telegram that we were to depart from Smolensk on July 4. But on the day of our impending departure, we received a telegram that read, "Postpone departure for Kursk. Lazarev." The telegram had been sent by our father's bodyguard.

Upon receiving the telegram, my mother understood that the worst had happened – my father had been arrested. She packed the rest of our things and a few hours later, our luggage was loaded into a truck. We – Mother, Leonid, Aunt Sonya and I – went to the railway terminal. Only my former nanny, Nyura, and her husband, a policeman who used to guard our house, came to see us off at the train station. Saying her farewell, Nyura hugged me tight and burst into tears. The train left and two hours later we arrived in Orsha, a railway-junction town to the west of Smolensk. In Orsha, we got off the train and bought tickets to Vinnitsa, where my mother's parents lived. That evening, my grandfather met us at the station, and as Leonid recalled, for the first time, he saw our mother cry. Probably this was the first time that she could allow herself to be weak, to relax after the nervous shock she had undergone. She knew that after our father's arrest, she would have to save all of us from deportation to Stalin's camps and the hardships of imprisonment. There had been no time for despair; she had had to pull herself together and find enough strength for immediate action. I can hardly remember that year, since I was only six years old, nor some of the following years, which I recollect as incomplete moments, though not associated with danger in my childish mind.

In June 1937, Stalin had initiated an unprecedented trial in which several outstanding military leaders were framed, ending with the execution of Uborevich, Tukhachevsky and Yakir, among others. Later, Ivan Konev and Georgy Zhukov, two leading Red Army marshals, wrote that Uborevich had an exceptional military talent and that his death was a terrible loss for the Soviet army. That same summer, the Soviet government, on the initiative of the Chief of the NKVD, Nikolai Ezhov, passed the Family Members of Traitors of the Motherland law, under which family members over the age of sixteen were arrested and sentenced to five to eight years of imprisonment and children were sent to special orphanages, where they were held under a strict regime. In many cases, the adults were, in fact, executed. This is why my father's bodyguard, Lazarev, had warned us not to come to Kursk.

Our father was arrested on July 3, 1937, the same day he got a new assignment (this "game" was a part of Stalin's style). We did not know anything about his fate for many years. In 1956, three years after Stalin's death, we received a statement about Father, which noted that he had died in January 1940. This was part of the posthumous rehabilitation of tens of thousands of people who had been executed during the repressions of the 1930s. A commemorative plaque with my father's name was placed on the house in Smolensk where we had lived.

In the 1980s, during Mikhail Gorbachev's policy of *glasnost*, openness, some archives were opened, and Father's case file became available. We learned that, in fact, he had been executed on October 29, 1937. Leonid spent a lot of time in libraries collecting documents about our father's activities and the tragic circumstances of his death, and he recorded the story of our parents and our life in those years.

Maybe it sounds cruel, but I thought then that it was probably better for my father, instead of suffering in prison until 1940. Even so, those four months spent in an underground cell of Lubyanka prison in Moscow must have been the most tragic of his life. Nowadays, we know how prisoners were treated there and what methods were used to obtain confessions of guilt from them. My brother said that in Leningrad in the 1970s, he met a man named Jacob Volshonok, who had been working as a secretary of the Military Court in those terrible times. He had drawn up the statements of cases and remembered October 29, 1937, very well, because on that day many important figures in the USSR were convicted and executed. Volshonok asked my brother what his father had looked like, and Leonid said that he had a beard. Volshonok then told him that all convicts were shaved right after being arrested and that he could not remember our father's trial as there had been about one hundred "trials" that day, one after another, a procedure that lasted three or four minutes for each person. Four minutes was enough to bring a prisoner from the underground cell, check his private papers, ask if he pleaded guilty and read a sentence. It was a death conveyor. There were no hearings, no lawyers. A sentence written beforehand was read out and the convict taken away. In the middle of the night, all prisoners were executed in Lubyanka. Our father was buried at Donskoy Cemetery in Moscow.

~

As I mentioned, there was a law subjecting a convict's family members to arrest and imprisonment. My brother wrote in his memoir, "Everybody I knew: Uborevich's wife and daughter, together with Rumyantsev's daughter, were imprisoned; Rumyantsev's son was executed." So how did we manage to survive?

All of our family escaped the lot of the others. Until her last days, my mother was confident that she had managed to trick the all-seeing NKVD. Everybody in Smolensk thought that we had gone to Kursk when, in fact, we had gone to Vinnitsa. The NKVD in Smolensk thought that their colleagues in Kursk would "take care" of us, and the Kursk department, in turn, believed that the Smolensk department must be in charge. So my mother thought. Probably this was the reason for our endless moving from Vinnitsa to Odessa, then back to Vinnitsa, several times in a row. However, my brother's explanation for why we were left untouched was quite different. In 1988, he found our father's file with a note on it – "Family members' law not to be applied" – signed by Leonid Zakovsky, who had become the head of the NKVD in Leningrad in 1934. I assume Zakovsky wrote this note because he had had feelings for my mother in his younger years. And though Zakovsky was himself executed in 1938, his signature remained in force and nobody could do any harm to us. Otherwise, our destinies could have been quite different.

~

In Vinnitsa, we moved into my grandfather's house, which had two apartments with two rooms in each. One room, which was attached to the kitchen, was vacant, and this is where my mother, brother and I lived. By country standards, Grandfather's house was rather large and comfortable, made of brick with an iron roof and wooden floors, although, like all other houses in the Old Town, it had no water supply or toilet. We had to pump water from the well in the yard, and the toilet was located in the garden, so we had to go outside any time of the year. Maybe because of that, I have immunity against the cold.

Finding ourselves in such conditions after two years of living in a mansion was not easy for my mother and brother; yet, despite all of these inconveniences, in comparison with the typical cob houses covered with thatched roofs, Grandfather's dwelling seemed very good to us. As for me, I was only six and didn't feel the inconvenience much. Besides, it was July and I spent most of the time in the yard or in the garden. But we didn't stay in Vinnitsa for long. Though a residency permit was required anywhere one lived, my mother didn't go to the town council office to get permission for permanent residence because she was afraid the authorities would look for her at her parents' place. So she decided to move to Odessa where her elder brother, Arkady, and two younger sisters, Nina and Betya, lived.

Arkady was an engineer who lived with his family in a proper apartment, while her sisters were students renting a tiny ten-square-metre room. It's hard to believe that my mother, my brother and I lived in the same room. Now I cannot even imagine how five people could manage to sleep there every night. In addition to these hardships, I got sick. Since my mother feared the authorities might find us in Odessa, the doctor who came to see me was not from a clinic but was, rather, one of our relatives. His name was Rabinovich, and I was told later that he was my father's brother. This is how I learned what my father's real last name was. My uncle was the only person from my paternal family I ever met. Mother had never told me about my father's family, and I guess my father himself did not want to keep in touch with them because they lived in Bessarabia, which then belonged to Romania. Having relatives living abroad caused suspicions and questioning from authorities at the time of Stalin's rule and long after that.

Doctor Rabinovich, my uncle, found that I had scarlet fever and sent me to the hospital. I was placed on a bed that had been occupied a day before by a child sick with measles, which I then caught in addition to scarlet fever. But this was not all; both diseases caused inflammation inside my ears and doctors were planning to do a trepanation, to make a hole in my skull to relieve pressure. I remember that the ward was on the first floor, and I could see my mother through the window, looking at me and crying. Even during very difficult moments I never saw tears in my mother's eyes, but this time the situation was terrible. She was in an illegal situation, threatened by arrest and exile, her daughter was near death and her son had left school at the age of fifteen and was working as a stevedore in the port of Odessa. This is how my brother recalled the time I was in the hospital:

I kept coming to the hospital every day, looking at your shaved head and sad eyes. You waved at me and I passed you some oranges that I'd gotten at the port of Odessa. Oranges were brought to Odessa by Spanish ships. At that time the war in Spain had already begun; ships would depart with soldiers and weapons and return with oranges. At first I was buying oranges from people who stole them, and then I decided I could steal them myself.

After a while my ear inflammation eased, an operation was no longer necessary and I got well. As I mentioned before, my father was idealistic and had a careless attitude toward our family's financial security. Therefore, after two months all my mother's savings ran out. Soon she got a job in the school canteen. I had nowhere to go because primary schools started at the age of eight, and I was only seven. Nevertheless, my mother begged the school principal to make an exception and, though classes had already started, I was admitted.

I was brought to the first-year group and took a seat at the desk. The first day in school should be fun for every student, but that day I didn't feel that way at all. I had no books or notebooks, I was not acquainted with the other children and I felt very uncomfortable. On the other hand, I could already read and count, so I adjusted quickly and everything soon seemed to be all right. Then summer vacation came and the same question arose: What to do with me? We rented a very small room in the most unpopular area of Odessa's slums, where living conditions were unbearable. Summer camps admitted children from the age of ten. And once again, my mother did her best: she persuaded a woman she knew, who was a cook in a summer camp, to take me with her.

This camp was located on the shore of the Black Sea and I remember it very well. During the daytime, I hung out with other children but at night I had to sleep with that woman, sharing the same bed. She put me to bed next to the wall and moved the bed slightly off the wall to gain some width, so I was hanging above the gap between the bed and the wall, clinging to the sheet all night long, trying not to fall into the gap. I also recall one older girl who had decided to teach me how to swim. Her teaching was based on a "well-known" method: leaving a child in deep water to either swim or drown. Unfortunately, I didn't show any ability for swimming and started to go under water. Luckily, there was a boy close to me who was a good swimmer, and he dragged me to the shore.

In 1939, Mother received a statement from Moscow that Father had been sentenced to ten years' imprisonment without the right to correspond with anyone. In the two-faced terms of Stalin's jurisdiction, it meant that he had been executed. But at that time, nobody knew the real meaning of such statements.

After receiving the notice from Moscow regarding my father's fate, we were able to get permission for permanent residence in Vinnitsa. Having nothing to lose, Mother decided to go back there. Luckily, finding accommodation in Vinnitsa was not a problem: we again lived at our grandfather's place. My grandparents gave their two rooms to us and moved to the extension – a kitchen and a small room – behind the house. This extension had a separate entrance from the garden. My uncle Boris now occupied the first apartment with his wife and son, who was two years younger than me. Boris was the only one among Grandfather's ten children who had stayed in the Old Town.

After two years of wandering and our troublesome existence in Odessa, our lives became more normal and secure. Mother got a position in the housekeeping department at the school, I was attending classes and Leonid got a job, too. He had left school – our father's arrest and the hardships that followed unsettled him for a long time, and Mother had no strength left to have any influence on him. Her main goals were to guard us against the danger we were in and to feed us. Nevertheless, I recall that period of my childhood as normal, when nothing unusual was happening. I missed my mother, who was at work all day long, but I had my grandparents. Lack of comfort and low living standards didn't mean anything to me; everybody around us lived the same way.

Like the majority of residents of the Old Town, my grandfather and grandmother spoke Ukrainian. They used Yiddish, too, but mostly to communicate between themselves or sometimes with their children. There were no Jews in the Old Town. All my friends were Ukrainian girls and boys and I learned their language quickly, but my mother tongue was Russian. The only school in the Old Town was Ukrainian, and the Russian school, where I was in Grade 3, was located on the far side of Vinnitsa. Every morning, I had to walk through the whole town, splashing through mud on rainy days. I studied well, and at the end of the school year I took part in an amateur play put on stage by our teacher, whose last name was Kirichenko. After the war, I studied at the same school as her daughter, Irina, and she became my dearest friend.

In summer, the Old Town was the best place for children: fruit orchards, the river and green meadows – all the pleasures of country life. All of my aunts and uncles, nine in number, used to bring their children to the Old Town during the summer, so I never felt lonely. I liked feeling that I belonged to a large family. I remember my grandfather cooking ears of corn in a *samovar* for his numerous grandchildren; we would stand in line holding plates in our hands and each of us would get two ears.

Sometimes Grandfather asked us to help in his garden and orchard, which was really enormous. The authorities did not take it away from him because he was growing new sorts of fruits and providing planting stock to Soviet agricultural communities. Every time he asked for help, we couldn't refuse, though our efforts suffered from our lack of enthusiasm. Usually, we collected black currants from the bushes that were planted along all the garden alleys. We also helped to pick up plums. Grandfather would shake the trees and we would gather falling plums into large baskets. It seems to me now that never in my life have I tasted such sweet and flavourful plums as those from my grandfather's orchard, although maybe it's just my imagination, remembering only the good things of my childhood.

Desperate Efforts

The summer of 1941, when I finished my third grade at school, started off as usual. But on June 22, the Germans crossed the western borders of the Soviet Union. Immediately after the declaration of war, my uncle Boris buried his family's most valuable belongings in the garden and left with his wife and son toward the east. Many Jews followed, fully understanding what was to come at the hands of the Nazis. But not everyone had a chance to flee – during the first days of war, the German troops advanced very quickly. At the beginning of the war, people just couldn't believe that the Germans would occupy vast territories of the USSR in a matter of days. There were a number of reasons why we couldn't make up our minds in time: first, there was my grandfather, whose age prevented him from making a quick decision; he couldn't leave his garden and orchard, which he had been growing with his own hands for more than twenty years. Also, my mother was tired after the years of wandering between Odessa and Vinnitsa, forced to hide in the wake of my father's arrest.

When it became obvious that further delay was not advisable, our family decided to leave. But it was too late. The trains were overcrowded and there wasn't room for ordinary people who had no privileges, as some high-ranking persons had. We stayed at the main railway station for several days trying to get on a train, but all our efforts failed. My aunt Sonya couldn't leave either. This was probably the most tragic page in our family's history. Aunt Sonya, my mother's elder sister, was beautiful, well educated, and had two daughters, Judith and Miriam, whom we used to call Ditha and Mira. The elder daughter, Ditha, was a real beauty; her portrait was featured at a local Vinnitsa photographer's exhibition. While a university student in Moscow, Ditha had married a very talented young engineer from Vinnitsa, Alexander Lerner. They had two daughters: five-year-old Inga and three-year-old Vita. At the beginning of the summer of 1941, Ditha had brought her daughters to her mother, who lived in Vinnitsa, and then went back to Moscow. Compared to Moscow, Vinnitsa seemed to be the countryside. Yet it was there that the two little girls were caught up in the war. I will never forget my aunt Sonya pacing back and forth on the platform of the train station in despair, trying to find some relative or friend who would agree to take the girls to Moscow and bring them back to their mother. But alas, nobody heeded her pleas; her desperate efforts were useless.

The only member of our family who managed to leave Vinnitsa was my brother, Leonid. When he joined us in our vain attempts to escape from the town, he wasn't alone. He brought a girl he was dating at that time, Dina Vainer. The atmosphere at the station was so tense that one of Mother's brothers made a scene, blaming Leonid for bringing a girlfriend at a time when the situation was so dangerous. Leonid took offense and left the station with Dina right away. They went east on foot, sometimes using passing horse carriages and military trucks, moving together with the retreating Red Army regiments. Leonid, eighteen at that time, was called up for the army soon after and Dina was left alone. She was pregnant and eventually gave birth to a baby boy.

After all our attempts to leave Vinnitsa failed, we returned to the Old Town. My aunt Sonya, her husband, Adya, and their granddaughters went back to their apartment in Vinnitsa.

The Germans were moving east rapidly. When it became clear that they were just about to enter the town and battles could break out in the streets, our family, as well as many of our neighbours, decided to hide in a large cellar overnight. No fewer than fifty people gathered there. We sat in complete darkness, terrified, waiting for the Germans to come. At dawn, we heard voices speaking German; somebody pounded at the cellar door with a rifle butt, yelling something in German. People inside whispered to one another until somebody ordered everyone to keep silent, explaining that the Germans probably suspected that Soviet soldiers were hiding inside the cellar, so we could expect a grenade to be thrown through the door. Silence settled immediately. For the first time in my life, I felt overwhelming bodily fear.

But the Germans moved on and in the morning we realized that the front line had passed the Old Town. Everybody came out of the cellar to a new reality – the Germans had occupied Vinnitsa. Since Grandfather had the best house in the Old Town, one of the German officers had moved in. Grandfather spoke Yiddish and probably some German, so he had a conversation with that officer, who confessed to not sharing Hitler's attitude toward Jews. After this conversation, my grandfather got very excited. He had never doubted the Nazis' plans regarding Jews, but now it looked like there was a sign of hope. It was short-lived.

Soon an order was issued forcing all Jews to wear a six-pointed star, the Star of David, sewn onto a sleeve. After that, when my mother went out, she would cover herself with a big shawl that covered the star as well; in this way she didn't show she was Jewish, yet she was not violating the order.

At the beginning of September 1941, the Germans made their first raid against the Jews of Vinnitsa. They went from door to door, taking men and young women away as if they were leaving for work. Since they did not conduct such a raid in the Old Town, many of us had the impression (absolutely false, as we soon realized) that the Old Town was safer to stay in. As the saying goes, a drowning man will clutch at a straw, so my aunt Sonya, her husband, Adya, and their two grand-daughters moved to our house in the Old Town. It was approximately one week before the "Final Solution to the Jewish problem" began in Vinnitsa. The tense atmosphere overwhelmed our family. One day, as five-year-old Inga sat next to me on the front steps of the house, she said, "Oh, Maya, I so badly don't want to be Jewish." I was only ten then, but I have remembered that phrase and Inga's sad eyes all my life. It seemed that Inga had a premonition of what her destiny would be.

The two rooms in our house that my uncle Boris and his family had occupied had remained empty since their escape from Vinnitsa during the first days of the war. At this time, a woman named Nyusya came with her three children from the town of Lvov to her mother, who was our nearest neighbour. Nyusya's husband had been recruited by the army, and she couldn't stay alone with her children. Since her mother's house was very small, my grandfather offered Nyusya the two empty rooms.

The situation in town grew more and more tense. At dawn one morning in mid-September 1941, a neighbour raised the alarm, informing us that screams had been heard at the boundary streets of the Old Town. The Germans were seen going from door to door, taking Jews. We thought they were taking young men and women to work, as they had done the week before. My mother asked Nyusya to take me to her rooms and rushed to the garden with Grandfather and Adya, Aunt Sonya's husband. Aunt Sonya stayed at home with her granddaughters because everybody thought that the Germans would not take old people and children for work. Nyusya put me in the same bed where her three children were sleeping. At that moment, the Germans came in, accompanied by a Ukrainian policeman. They asked Nyusya what nationality she was. Frightened to death, with her hands shaking, she showed them her Ukrainian passport. As the Germans pointed to the children Nyusya told them, "These are my children." With that decisive statement, this brave woman saved my life. The Germans left, heading to the house extension where Aunt Sonya and her granddaughters were. In a few minutes, they were brought out. I could see through the window that they hadn't been allowed to put on proper clothes. Sonya carried the younger girl, Vita, who was wearing only a short nightgown.

That day, Nyusya took her children and me and we all moved to her mother's house. Knowing nothing about my mother's fate, I stayed with Nyusya for two or three days more. Meanwhile, the news spread across Vinnitsa that the Germans had taken at least ten thousand Jews out of town to the nearest forest, where a huge trench was dug; all of them were executed there. There were many wounded, as well as children, who were thrown in the trench alive, buried together with the dead. People said that for several days it looked like the earth was moving.

After two days, Nyusya made it clear to me that she was afraid to keep me any longer. The only thing I could do was try to find my mother. I decided to look for her at the homes of her close friends. First I went to Maria Khomichuk, who lived in the Old Town. When I asked her if my mother was there, she looked frightened and answered that she knew nothing about her whereabouts. I headed further into the Old Town, going into many houses, but all my efforts were worthless. As I passed through almost all the streets of Vinnitsa, it was getting dark and I was scared. In spite of my young age, I understood why Nyusya refused to keep me any longer, but I had no idea where else to go. Walking down the street toward the bridge leading to the Old Town, I stopped near the park and began to cry in despair. When complete darkness fell, I got so frightened that I had no choice but to go back to Nyusya. To my great joy, my mother was waiting for me there! She was very worried about me because she knew I had left the house in the morning. I found out that my mother had been at Maria's but that Maria had been afraid to tell me because she did not want to let Mother's whereabouts become known to anyone. What a horrific time it was!

Soon my mother learned that Grandmother had been taken with Aunt Sonya, Inga and Vita, but Grandfather had managed to escape the raid and was hiding in the attic of his neighbour's house. Mother had a chance to see him one last time; a few days later, we heard that he had hanged himself from a pear tree in his orchard. He was taken out of the noose and buried by his close friend, Piotr Andrievsky. Apparently, the neighbour who saved him from the raid had refused to keep him in the attic anymore. My grandfather probably committed suicide not just out of despair and hopelessness but because he felt guilty for having delayed our evacuation from Vinnitsa. It may sound cruel, but when I recall the three years my mother and I spent under German occupation, I think my grandfather made the right decision.

Only those who did not have "typical" Jewish features and could speak without the slightest Yiddish accent had a chance of surviving. Moreover, someone had to be as brave and energetic as my mother in order to constantly move from place to place. My grandfather decided to put an end to all future suffering because he knew he would not be able to survive. I later learned that Sonya's husband, Adya, also hanged himself.

Finally, late that night, my mother took me by the hand and we returned to Maria Khomichuk's house. We spent only a few days there. Maria had two children and didn't want to take the risk of hiding us in her house. I don't remember if the Germans had already announced that they would execute anyone trying to save Jews, but everybody knew of the executions near Vinnitsa and nobody doubted that they would pay with their lives for helping Jews. It was dangerous to stay in Maria's house, so every night Mother and I went to the forest. Since it was already October, nights were cold and my mother covered me with the dark blue shawl she had taken with her at dawn when the first raid had begun. My mother understood that we wouldn't be able to remain this way for long and that we needed some shelter. She found another friend in the Old Town, a woman who agreed to take us in. This woman had a six-year-old child, who could easily reveal to the neighbours who we were, so she placed us in a dark corridor where nobody usually walked. I remember lying on the floor of that corridor all day long, listening to the voices of children playing in the yard. I had a strong wish to play with them, but at age ten I understood very well why we had to hide. Two or three weeks later, her child discovered us and we had to leave again. I didn't want to leave this very uncomfortable place because I knew that our every movement was associated with mortal danger – in the Old Town, everybody knew us.

Fortunately, my mother had many friends, not only among Jews. On the other bank of the Southern Bug River in Vinnitsa, she found her friend Olga and asked her for help. Olga lived in a small one-family house. As I recall, she was a good-looking woman in her forties. She lived together with her niece, a young woman who had a baby. The young woman's husband had been a fighter pilot who was killed on the front line during the first days of war. Although she already knew this, both women had resigned themselves to the new situation pretty quickly. German officers started to come to their house very often; even at my young age, I found it unacceptable that a young woman who had lost her husband a few months before could amuse herself with German officers. Yet, though it may sound like a paradox, because of the German presence, Olga's house was safer for us than any other place. My mother played the role of a housemaid, cooking and serving meals. I hid in the house so as not to show my face, recognizable as Jewish, to anybody. But for a long time, the situation was very risky, and it eventually became unbearable.

After a while, it seemed like my mother had exhausted every possibility in asking her friends for shelter; soon there was no one left to ask. Still, my mother made another desperate attempt. As I mentioned, Leonid's girlfriend, Dina Vainer, had gone with him on foot from Vinnitsa before the Germans came. Dina's father, Ilya Vainer, an educated person with an easy temper, had been a pharmacy manager before the war; Dina's mother had died a few years earlier. The pharmacy was not far from Olga's house, and my mother went there to learn about Ilya's fate. She found out that he had not managed to leave either. When the first anti-Jewish raid began, the cleaner at the pharmacy, a woman named Marfusha, hid him in her house. I think this woman deserves to be called a hero. Not only did Marfusha save Ilya from the raid during the first days of occupation, she kept him for three years in the cellar under the floor of her room! The room was part of a small storage area in the back of the pharmacy. In small Ukrainian houses, such cellars were used as cold rooms where food supplies were kept during the summer. Access to the cellar was through an opening in the floor, which had a cover, and inside the cellar there was a ladder. In summer, at night, Ilya climbed up the ladder and sat in a room near the open window, but he never walked out into the yard.

When my mother came to Marfusha, this kind woman told her everything and agreed to give us shelter in the same cellar. When we first went down the ladder and I saw a small man with a large black beard, I felt out of sorts, but I soon realized that Ilya's way of life hardly required shaving. But we didn't stay there for long. Either Marfusha was not able to keep all of us – after all, she had to feed us – or my mother realized that this existence could not be maintained.

Since we had nowhere else to go in Vinnitsa, we had to leave. It was too dangerous for my mother to show up on the town's streets, where anybody could recognize her. We needed papers to move to another town, which meant that Mother had to have a passport with a record confirming that her nationality was Russian. Some people advised my mother to apply at the police station and claim that just before the beginning of the war she had given in her passport to be exchanged for a new one, which she had never received. Such cases were not unusual, but five witnesses were required. Three people were found at once – Maria Khomichuk, Olga and her niece. After a while, Mother found another two; I suspect she simply paid them.

Mother finally received a passport that identified her as Ortho-dox and Russian, with the patronymic name changed from Moisey (Moses) to Michael. My name was changed from Maya to Maria.

With this passport, we were ready to go. However, before our departure from Vinnitsa, my mother showed, once again, how determined and courageous she could be.

Our grandfather had not been rich, but like many people, he liked to put some money aside. Being a prudent person, he had saved, instead of bank notes, pre-revolution golden five-ruble coins. When the Germans came, he had buried a small box with the coins in his garden and had shown the place to my mother. When we were ready to leave Vinnitsa, she decided to take the extreme risk of going back to our house to retrieve the money. Even though German officers and soldiers already occupied our house, Mother had the courage to go to our garden at night and dig the box out.

We then set out for the small town of Pogrebishche, where Olga's relative gave us shelter. I hardly remember this time, probably because, to avoid being seen by neighbours, I never went out to the street. It was much simpler for my mother, whose features were not "typically" Jewish. Even after the war, my mother would be given such "compliments" as "You have a very good appearance – you don't look Jewish!"

We spent two winter months in Pogrebishche. Our host had no children and I got used to being alone. My main goal was to be unseen – all the rest didn't matter. One day, somebody in the house stoked a wood stove and closed the choke too early. I was so badly poisoned by the fumes that I lost consciousness and my mother had to carry me out into the yard. It was in the middle of the day, and because the neighbours saw this entire scene, we had to change our whereabouts again for fear they might report that the host of the house was hiding Jews.

The next day we left for Kazatin (now Koziatyn, Ukraine). It seemed we had nowhere else to go; we spent two days at the railroad station. My mother put me in a dark corner, bundling my face in her large shawl. Finally, a man wearing a railway worker's uniform noticed us and invited us to his house, perhaps taking pity on a woman with a child. When I found myself in his kitchen I felt as though I was in a palace. It was so warm and bright, and I had been hidden in dark corners for so long that I had forgotten how bright a house could be. We were served hot pancakes right from the frying pan; it was *Maslenitsa*, cheese-fare week, the time before Lent when dairy foods were still permitted. Later, in memory of those days, I began to celebrate cheese-fare week. I would invite guests and propose a toast to the railway worker of Kazatin. To my regret, I don't remember his name or the names of many others who helped us in those difficult times.

We didn't stay in Kazatin for long. Our goal was to pass into the territory occupied by Romanian troops. Romania was an ally of Germany and the Germans had transferred Transnistria, an area which had been part of Ukraine, to Romanian control. Yet, we had heard rumours that Romanians were not as zealous in tracking down Jews. In one village, Mother found a countryman who agreed to transport us on his carriage to the territory under Romanian control.

In the spring of 1942, we found ourselves in Vapniarka, which was part of Transnistria between October 1941 and March 1944. My mother got a job as a housemaid with the family of a railway worker, whose wife was about to give birth. I spent a terrible night listening to the screaming of the woman in labour. But everything went well – the baby was delivered, and my mother had obviously been a great help. A bit later, Mother rented a room for us nearby and kept working for that family. In this new situation, she was not able to hide me anymore and, in spite of my Jewish appearance, I started to live more or less the normal life of a country girl. I even had friends with whom I played in the yard. It was summertime and schools were closed, if they still existed in wartime.

We lived in Vapniarka for several months, and it was here that my mother met a woman who made my continued survival possible. The woman's name was Anna Mikheyeva, and she had come from Odessa with her close friend, Linda. My mother's first glance at Linda was enough to make her realize that the woman was Jewish. In turn, Anna looked at me and guessed the same thing. She told my mother a terrible story about how the Germans had killed Linda's mother in front of her. Somehow, Linda had managed to avoid execution, but she had suffered a terrible nervous breakdown. Anna decided to leave Odessa with Linda for some other place, thinking it would be the best way to bring her some peace. Probably they had friends in Vapniarka and that was the reason why they came to town. Linda was a German-language teacher, and as soon as she had recovered enough, Anna helped her find a position as a translator with a German regiment quartered in Vapniarka. Sometimes such reckless or even crazy steps actually resulted in survival. And then something absolutely unbelievable happened. A German officer, a captain serving in that regiment – I remember him well; he had an intellectual face and was not tall – fell in love with Linda, and it looked like she loved him in return. When the regiment had to change location, Linda went with her officer. Maybe she just had no choice.

Anna decided to return to Odessa, and before she left she said to my mother, "It will be very difficult for both of you to survive together. I can take your girl with me to Odessa if you want." And my mother agreed.

Then we faced another problem: my documents. My name was written in my mother's new passport, which was, in fact, a fake. We didn't have any other documents, but again my mother found a solution. In Soviet times, the majority of children weren't baptized. After the Germans came, many churches were reopened in occupied territories, and almost every grandmother wanted her grandchildren to be baptized. It was common for grown-up children to undergo baptism and so, believe it or not, I was baptized, too. According to the rite, a child must be lifted above the ground; I remember that the old priest could hardly lift me since I was eleven years old. But the main goal was reached: I got a document I needed badly, and Anna and I headed to Odessa.

On the way there was an incident that I remember as if it happened yesterday. When the train stopped at a station, a Romanian policeman came in and, passing through the car, looked at me and said, "Hey, you, Jewish child, what are you doing here?" Then he thought for a moment and added, "I will be back for you!" And he walked away. I cannot recall why Anna was not near me; probably there were a lot of passengers and she had gone to the next car. I didn't know where she was and got very frightened. I understood what danger I was in and a stream of thoughts kept running through my head: What to do? Stay where I was? But the policemen said he was going to be back for me. Get off the train at the next station? I could get lost. Go and fetch Anna? I could run into the same policeman. I really didn't know what to do. At this desperate moment, I started to ask for help from God: I prayed. I had been brought up in an absolutely atheistic family, but while I was in Vapniarka, a girl had taught me prayers she had learned from her grandmother. I guess the Lord heard my prayers – the Romanian policeman never came back for me. Thus, I had proof of the rumour that Romanians were less zealous than Germans regarding the annihilation of Jews. At the same time, I frankly believed that God had heard me. Later, when I lived in Odessa, I kept praying in the morning, which caused Anna some embarrassment and aroused her derision.

Hiding in the Open

Anna had a luxurious apartment in Odessa, a spacious five rooms with a large kitchen and a bathroom. It was in one of the most prestigious districts of the city, at the corner of Gogol Street and Sabaneiv Bridge Street near the famous Odessa Conservatory. Anna had gotten this amazing dwelling from the Germans. Before the war, she had lived in a good building but had had only one room. When the Germans came, they took up this building for some important office and the tenants were all offered other apartments.

There were a lot of abandoned dwellings in Odessa at that time, as many high-ranking people had fled the city. I don't remember if Anna owned the whole apartment or only a major part of it: two large living rooms and a kitchen with a maid's room in the back. There were two smaller rooms with windows facing the so-called rectangular well, formed by the walls of other tall buildings. One of the rooms was occupied by a woman who lived alone. I don't remember her name. She was silent most of the time and never talked to neighbours; people suspected she worked with the Siguranța, the Romanian secret police. A Polish woman named Teophilia Philipovna lived in the second room; she also was alone but was frank and cordial, and treated me very well. Before the war she had been a housekeeping manager in the most prestigious hotel at the seaside of Odessa. Teophilia taught me laundering, ironing and other housekeeping skills. She often took me to the Catholic Church, especially during holidays. Sometimes she invited me for dinner, and her soups were so delicious! My guardian, Anna, didn't like to cook at all and our meals were rather meagre. Teophilia noticed that and decided to feed me. I believe she suspected who I was by birth and tried to make my life a little easier.

I have often asked myself, What did our neighbours think of me? I lived at Anna's openly and everybody knew that I was not her daughter. I don't remember what kind of history was presented to our neighbours, but I do remember one episode from that time. One day, a woman who lived in the same house came to us, asking Anna to help her kill a live hen for dinner. Anna answered that she was not able to do it but that her Marusya (that was me) would. I was horrified but couldn't refuse. Luckily, I had once seen how women did this, so I took that miserable hen to the shed and cut her throat. When the woman left, Anna explained to me why she had insisted that I kill the hen. Doing this job, she said, would dispel suspicions that I was a Jewish child. I believe such rumours and suspicions were circulating but nobody betrayed me; on the contrary, everybody treated me well.

The first winter I spent in Odessa was difficult. I had no warm clothes to wear and Anna did not work and consequently was hard-pressed for money. Most of the time, our main meal was *galushki*, cooked dough balls made of coarse dark flour. Maybe Anna's culinary abilities were just limited; she really hated to cook. However, our situation soon improved significantly, as Anna got a position as a chemistry teacher in a new *Gymnasium*, high school, that was founded by a lady who had emigrated from Soviet Russia after the revolution and then came back to Odessa from Romania. Children whose parents had suffered under the Soviet authorities had a priority entering classes. So Anna taught chemistry and, at the same time, was a leading tutor of graduate students, while I spent my days at home because I was not yet allowed to show myself in public.

Meanwhile, my mother moved from Vapniarka to Kotovsk (called Birzula at that time), which had a railway junction station. Mother got a job as a housekeeper for a Romanian office worker. From time to time, she came to Odessa to see me, but she never came to Anna's. She would stay in an apartment at the far end of Odessa near Privoz, the famous market, and I would walk through the whole city to meet with her. Probably at the beginning, Anna accompanied me on my trips, but after a while, I did them by myself. On my way, I had a chance to see and explore this beautiful town and its attractions. Though I lived there for only a couple of years, and in such difficult and dangerous times, the impression Odessa left on me has stayed with me all my life.

Undoubtedly, my mother provided Anna with money for me. Even in those difficult times, she found a way to earn some extra money. Every time she came to Odessa, she would buy candies at a small private factory and then sell them in Birzula. She called this business "reimbursement of travel expenses."

In the summer of 1943, a strange event took place that I still cannot explain. The doorbell rang one day and Anna went to the door, which had a chain, and half opened it. An unknown young man said quietly in Russian with a slight foreign accent, "I have a letter for you from Linda." Anna let him in with joy – after all, she hadn't heard from Linda since she had left Vapniarka – and showed him into the room, where they sat at the table to talk. The young man had come from Poland and said he was in Odessa temporarily on business with a group of people. He asked Anna's permission to stay for a few days, and she agreed. The next day, he settled in one of the vacant rooms, and immediately after that his friends came to see him – mostly young men, some of them wearing German military uniforms. Everything felt strange but we preferred not to ask any questions. A few days passed and our guest left. After a while, he came back and asked for lodging again, this time for a couple of days. I don't remember if he brought any news from Linda, but Anna let him in again. After he left, an elderly man came and occupied the room, staying inside most of the time. In the evenings, he would come into the kitchen and have long conversations with Anna. She suspected he was Jewish. He stayed with us no more than a week, but a few days after he left, we noticed that we were being watched.

All day long a police spy stood under our balcony and as soon as Anna or I left the house, he followed us. It was very unpleasant, and we could not guess for what purpose it was done. Then, late one night, Siguranţa men broke into our apartment and began a search. Though nothing was found, they arrested Anna and took her with them. I waited until dawn and, in the morning, rushed to a close friend of Anna's who lived rather far from our place. I told her what had happened and asked her to prepare a parcel for Anna because I wanted to go immediately to the Siguranţa jail and visit her. After all, I owed her my life; how could I leave her alone at this time?

Even now, I cannot understand how that woman let me go to the Siguranţa by myself. Being Anna's closest friend, didn't she know or suspect my nationality? But she didn't say a word; she just prepared a small parcel with food and I headed to the Siguranţa office. There, someone who appeared to be important questioned me. He looked through the parcel, returned the fork and knife to me, explaining that prisoners were not allowed to have them, and left the food. This officer was very polite with me, perhaps expecting to get some additional information from me. All his questions were about our recent guests from Poland. Most likely, the Siguranţa did not have any interest in me, even if they did have a notion of who I might be. So I returned to Anna's friend.

I understood that I would not be able to live alone, so I went to the house where my mother and I usually met. From there, I sent this alarming news to her in Birzula. My mother was horrified and left for Odessa immediately. But the whole story ended quite unexpectedly. Anna was freed late the following night and even brought to her place by car. Later, Anna told me that the Siguranţa had interrogated her, asking her to tell them everything she knew about the men staying in her apartment. Anna supposed that the elderly man, the last one who lived in her apartment and with whom she'd had long conversations, was being held by the Siguranţa at the same time. Moreover, she contended that she heard him screaming as if he was being tortured. It seemed that either the Siguranţa understood that Anna had nothing in common with those men or it was enough that she had agreed to co-operate with them.

There could be one other explanation: Anna had a sister, who, although not young, was a very beautiful woman with an intelligent face. She kept herself in good shape, was always well dressed, and she looked like a real lady. Anna once told me that her sister was the lover of the Romanian public prosecutor of Odessa. Probably she assisted in Anna's release. Whatever happened, it remains a mystery for me.

In the autumn of 1943, Anna decided to enroll me in the *Gymnasium* where she worked. Undoubtedly, this decision was made with my mother's consent. Nobody knew what was more dangerous – staying at home would prompt the question of why I wasn't attending classes while Anna worked at the *Gymnasium*, and attending classes would expose my face to many people.

I was enrolled in the first class, which required four years of primary school. I had only three years but had never had a problem with school. Besides, I was so happy to go to school again and to be together with other children that it gave me a strong motivation for learning. My favourite subject was religion, maybe because it was new for me. Though my belief in God, inspired by the incident on the train, had already faded, I attended religious classes willingly.

Unfortunately, the fact that I had started to live openly made my life more dangerous. One day, a young friend of Anna's, a former student who had become an artist, approached Anna with the idea of drawing me; since she was painting a canvas representing a religious episode, she needed Jewish faces and considered my face quite appropriate. We were all horrified and tried to persuade her to give up this bad idea. To make sure our refusal would not cause any unwarranted suspicions, Anna's good friend, a doctor, placed me in a hospital for three weeks.

Meanwhile, in order to improve her financial situation, Anna decided to rent one of her two large rooms to a Romanian officer. I cleaned the room and waxed the parquet floors. When everything was ready, the Romanian major settled in with his attending soldier, who was a good fellow. He came into our kitchen quite often and established friendly relations with us. As for our major, he didn't waste his time. Every night, a different young and beautiful woman would visit him. The whole week was scheduled this way and the officer played the role of chief coordinator.

One day, the soldier came to us with a box of chocolate candies and some news. The major was expecting his wife to visit from Bucharest, and according to the soldier, she was rich and influential. We were urgently asked not to tell this lady that other women were visiting her husband. We had no intention of telling her anything. Besides, when the major's wife came, she didn't pay much attention to us. As for the major, he started treating us very respectfully and politely. As a matter of fact, as soon as bad news from the front line started to come in and it became clear that the Germans and their allies were losing the war, our tenant's attitude toward us grew even more respectful.

Return to Life

At the beginning of the spring of 1944, it was obvious that the German troops were retreating. At that time, it was forbidden to have or to listen to shortwave radios and so we didn't have one in the apartment. Yet there were people who, in spite of the strict prohibition, did listen to shortwave broadcasts and then spread the news among friends and neighbours. At the end of March, when the front line approached Odessa, my mother left Birzula and came to us. She feared that we could find ourselves on opposite sides of the front line. A week before Odessa was freed, my mother appeared in Anna's apartment openly, no longer anxious that somebody would report her when Soviet troops were so close.

With the front line approaching, the citizens of Odessa worried that, before leaving, the Germans would blow up the famous Odessa Opera House, of which everybody was very proud. Crowds of people gathered near the building, ready to extinguish a fire in case of an explosion. The house we lived in was close to the residence of the Romanian military governor of Odessa, and on the other side of the building there were German barracks. On the day when German and Romanian authorities started to act as if they had only hours left to stay in town, all the tenants from our house, fearing being bombed, moved to the air-raid shelter in the building on the next street, where a lot of people gathered. We spent the whole night in the shelter. At dawn on April 10, the Soviet army entered Odessa. We greeted the soldiers with great joy; for my mother and me it was really a coming back to life. I remember the faces of our liberators: weary, and at the same time, joyful and cordial.

As soon as Soviet troops entered the town, we returned to Anna's apartment on Gogol Street. Despite our worries, no serious damage was done to the building; a small calibre shell had hit the building's corner and destroyed only one apartment. However, by some quirk of fate, the building where we had spent the night in the shelter was hit by a bomb that broke through all the floors and exploded in the first-floor apartment. Not long before that, my close friend's grandmother had brought all of her family jewels to that apartment. My friend's name was Nadya, and she lived in our neighbourhood at the beginning of Sabaneiv Bridge Street in a beautiful house decorated with colour mosaics, a picture of which was included in many books about Odessa. As Nadya told me once, this house had belonged to her grandfather. After the revolution, the authorities took it away and left her grandfather one apartment on the first floor. I used to visit that apartment frequently. Nadya actually lived in Leningrad with her parents, but in the summers, they brought her to Odessa. In the summer of 1941, when the war began, Nadya was cut off from her parents. As far as I remember, Nadya's grandmother looked much younger than her grandfather. According to Nadya's story, she was her grandfather's second wife, a former singer or a dancer in some *café chantant*, entertaining customers in an outdoor coffee shop. Nadya's grandmother stuffed all their family jewels into a suitcase and hid it in the apartment before all of them went down to the same air-raid shelter. The bomb I mentioned destroyed everything. It was a misfortune, but the real disaster came later: Nadya learned that her parents had died during the blockade of Leningrad.

When the Germans retreated from Odessa, they set fire to their barracks, which were close to the house where Nadya lived with her grandparents. The flames spread to the upper floor of the house. It was my mother who again showed her management skills. Although she was new to the neighbourhood, unknown to anybody, she organized people into a chain to pass buckets of water to the upper floor and, in this way, the flames were extinguished quickly.

After Odessa was freed, I rushed immediately to the Palace of Young Pioneers, a youth centre for schoolchildren. It was located in the former Duke Vorontsov Palace at Primorsky (Seaside) Boulevard. I still had memories of the pre-war amateur performance I had taken part in and enrolled in the amateur theatre group right away. But we didn't stay in Odessa for long; in the middle of May 1944, we left for Kiev. One of my mother's brothers, Senya, who had not been recruited into the army because of health problems, had lived in Kiev before the war and returned there after the Red Army liberated it in November 1943. During the war, Odessa was much less destroyed than Kiev. When I saw Khreshchatyk, the main and the most beautiful street of Kiev, it was completely ruined. It made a terrible impression on me. We rented a room at the far end of the city and lived there for a few months. In the autumn, we went back to my grandfather's house in Vinnitsa.

Before the war, many members of the Brik family and their numerous relatives had been living in the city of Odessa. After Ukraine was liberated, those family members who had survived – including my mother's siblings Arkady, Betya and Boris – for some reason did not go back to Odessa, and instead one by one returned to our house in Vinnitsa. I remember that at the beginning, I didn't like the atmosphere there. First of all, every single thing in Grandfather's house and the Old Town reminded me of tragedy. Secondly, I had been living under Nazi occupation for three years and therefore, my psyche and my way of thinking had changed. I was only thirteen, and I had become aware that being Jewish was deadly dangerous. I declared to my mother that I wanted to keep my new Russian name, Marusya, and I didn't want to live among Jewish people anymore. Fortunately, all those feelings faded soon and things sorted themselves out.

Before the war, my school studies had continued for only three years; then, in Odessa, I had attended classes in the *Gymnasium* for six months. In Vinnitsa, in the autumn of 1944, I became a Grade 6 student. The atmosphere at school was easy, but the classrooms were missing desks – students sat at small tables, and those who had no tables sat on the floor and leaned against the wall.

In Vinnitsa, we got wonderful news – my brother, Leonid, was alive! He had survived in the army, though he had been wounded in battle twice. Dina Vainer, whom he had married, soon came to Vinnitsa with their three-year-old son, Alik. When I saw Alik for the first time, I felt that my brother was looking at me; they were so remarkably alike!

Life in Vinnitsa gradually returned to normal. Obviously it remained difficult because the war was still going on elsewhere, but we were inspired by the good news coming from the front line: our troops were moving to the West. The best news, for my mother and me, was that we were not hiding anymore for the sake of our lives.

Epilogue

We remained in Vinnitsa until the end of the war. Victory Day was the greatest holiday in my life and I will remember it forever. But, as one song says, for many of us, it was a "teary-eyed" holiday.

We continued living in Grandfather's house in the Old Town. But of course, my mother's sisters and brothers saw the house as an inheritance meant for all of his children. It was decided that the house would be sold, and the money received from the sale would be divided among all the heirs. I don't remember the exact sum, but it was enough to buy one room in the city of Chernivtsi, where we subsequently moved. We chose Chernivtsi for several reasons. Before the war, it belonged to Romania, but after the war it became part of Ukraine. Because many locals didn't want to live under Soviet power and were leaving the city for Romania, the prices of private houses were understandably lower there than in other cities. Moreover, two of my mother's brothers had already moved to Chernivtsi with their families. The big room we bought was located in an apartment with a shared kitchen in a fairly small one-storey house. Compared to Vinnitsa, these conditions seemed luxurious to us. The house was close to the city centre and it had plumbing, a bathtub and a toilet. My school was nearby, so there was no need to trudge through mud for miles, like in Vinnitsa. The Palace of Pioneers was also nearby, and I immediately joined its drama club. An actor from the local drama theatre led the club, and I dedicated more time to learning my roles than to my studies. In Chernivtsi, there was a decent drama theatre, which I visited often. It was around this time that the desire to become an actress ripened within me.

After the war, Leonid decided to stay in the military, becoming an officer. By the time I graduated high school he was living and serving in the military unit on the outskirts of Leningrad.

Despite the fact that I dedicated so much time to the drama club, I finished high school with very good grades. Having received my certificate of secondary education, I decided to move to Leningrad to apply to the theatre institute. But my dreams were not that easy to realize. Upon arrival, I immediately went to the theatre institute to find out about the conditions for admission. It turned out that the competition was fierce: for each spot, there were about twenty applicants. I realized that in this situation, my chances of getting admitted were very low. I met a young man there who told me that he had already taken the institute's entrance exams two years in a row and had not gotten in, and if he failed again that year, he would try to enter the Bonch-Bruevich Leningrad Electro-Technical Institute of Communications. That institute's drama club was led by a professional theatre director, and it had won first prize in the competition of drama club productions among Leningrad institutions of higher education three years in a row. And there were many such institutions in Leningrad. On learning about this opportunity, I also decided to apply for this institute. It turned out that admissions there were also competitive – though it was only four people for every spot. And I was not scared of their core exams in physics and mathematics, since these subjects always came easily to me. I passed the exams successfully, and I was accepted to the Faculty of Radio and Television.

Of course, as soon as classes started, I set out at once to join the drama club, where I immediately got a role in Ostrovsky's *Guilty Without Fault*. This was a role for a character actor, and the student who used to play it had graduated and left Leningrad. My life in the institute was fairly typical; coursework came easily to me and I liked it. I usually passed my exams with excellent marks and received an increased stipend for two semesters. This stipend was awarded to those who passed all their exams with excellent marks. I spent the first half of my day in courses, and the second in drama club rehearsals.

At the time I lived in a very small room with Leonid and his family, but unfortunately the commute to the institute took over an hour by tram. Yet there was a different matter that was of more concern to me. Before I started with college applications, when filling out questionnaire forms back in grade school I would admit that my father had been arrested in 1937. But when I arrived in Leningrad and was accepted into the institute, my brother warned me not to write about my father's arrest in questionnaires, since he kept it a secret. So for four years, until Stalin's death in 1953, I was afraid that I would be exposed. But, fortunately, nothing of the sort happened. Apparently, by that time, no one was paying attention to these things.

In my fourth year at the institute, I met Lucjan, a student from Poland who was in the same year of studies there. We fell in love and decided to marry. Fortunately, this was after Stalin's death, and marriages with foreigners, which had been forbidden, were now allowed. In 1954, when we graduated from the institute, my husband was supposed to return to Warsaw, while I stayed in Leningrad awaiting a permit to go abroad. This was a very difficult period in my life. It turned out that I was pregnant. Usually in such cases the permit arrived in two or three months, but I had waited for six months and there was still no response. Eventually, my husband made an appeal to the Soviet Embassy in Warsaw, requesting clarification of the reason for the delay. That worked, and after seven months of waiting, I arrived in Warsaw. Our daughter Irina was born in April 1955 in Warsaw. My mother, who had in the meantime moved from Chernivtsi to Leningrad, would come to visit us. She helped me raise Irina, and I got a job in my field. But I did not feel at home in Poland at the time, so in 1956 my husband and I decided to return to Leningrad, at least for a while.

My husband had been invited to apply for PhD studies at the same institute, and I got a job there. While we were in Poland, my mother had bought a small room with a kitchen in Porokhovye, on the outskirts of Leningrad, and when we returned to Leningrad we lived with her. After Lucjan finished his PhD studies and defended his dissertation in 1961, we went back to Warsaw. There, I got a job at the Radio and Television Project Bureau. I liked the work a lot; it was interesting and the salary was high. I was engaged in the planning of television networks for the whole of Poland.

We bought a co-operative apartment in the city centre, and life went on as usual. Our second daughter, Paulina, was born in 1964. After maternity leave I returned to work, and a housekeeper took care of the household and the children.

In March 1968, an antisemitic campaign began in Poland. Most of the remaining Jews were now leaving the country. I believed that we also needed to leave. However, my husband was against taking this step. I didn't insist, because I understood that I wouldn't be able to find a comparably good job elsewhere. We stayed in Warsaw, and I continued working in that same project bureau.

At the end of the 1970s, my husband got a Doctor of Science degree. His work situation became more complicated, and this time he decided that we needed to leave Poland. Before then, he had gone twice to universities in the US and Canada as a visiting scholar for a year, and he hoped that he wouldn't have any problems getting a job in either country. In early 1981, we submitted a claim stating that we wanted to leave Poland for Israel, since it was easier for Jews to get an exit permit to go there. For me, this turned out to be one of the most difficult periods in my life. My mother, then eighty-two, stayed in Leningrad; she died there in 1984. My eldest daughter, Irina, was already married, and her husband would not hear of leaving Poland. The youngest, Paulina, was sixteen; she couldn't stay on her own, of course, but she didn't want to leave either. And I was leaving a wonderful job, realizing that at my age, and with an insufficient knowledge of English, I might have big problems getting a job. It's not surprising that in such a situation I found myself depressed.

Within a few months, we got an exit permit and left Poland. Since we were planning to go not to Israel but to Canada, we stayed in Ladispoli near Rome. This was where Jews who were not going to Israel waited for visas for the US or Canada to be issued. On average, a permit to enter the US came within a month, but you had to wait two or three months for a Canadian permit. We, however, didn't get an answer for six months. In this situation, my depression only got worse. Finally, seven months later, we received visas to enter Canada.

At the end of 1981, we went to Montreal, where Lucjan's cousin lived, and where he had previously worked as a professor at McGill University for a year.

Upon our arrival, my husband got a job in his field very quickly, and Paulina went to school. We initially rented an apartment, but within a year we bought a small house in the suburbs.

Not everything went smoothly with my employment. At first, to my great surprise, I was hired by the Canadian Broadcasting Corporation (CBC). After all, at the time I was already fifty-two, my English was weak and, moreover, this was a highly competitive position. But during the interview, they realized that I had a lot of experience in this field, and apparently this played a positive role. I was involved in designing the television network for the whole of Canada. However, a year and a half later there was a lot of downsizing in the organization, and I lost my job, but I didn't linger at home for long. In CBC's engineering department, I was told that the Russian section of Radio Canada International, which was part of the corporation, was looking for an employee who could prepare the material for the show and afterwards deliver it into the microphone – in short, a radio journalist. Initially, I decided that this job was not for me because I had never had anything to do with this type of work. But my friends convinced me, and I applied for the position. A couple of weeks later, I was invited for an interview, during which I had to translate an English text into Russian and then read it into the microphone. And, again, to my surprise, I was invited to work there. This is where my passion for theatre and my participation in drama clubs in my youth came in handy. That's where I developed good diction. It turned out that my voice worked well with radio, and I had always been interested in political issues. I really liked the work, despite the fact that I had to catch the train at 6:20 a.m.

At first I mostly prepared the news and press reviews, but later on I was invited to prepare an original program for DXers, which is the term for shortwave radio enthusiasts. This is where my background in radio engineering came in handy. This program was a great success, and I received many letters from listeners.

I worked for seventeen years and retired at age seventy-two. Having more time available, I started to look into having both my mother's friend Maria Khomichuk and Anna Mikheyeva named as Righteous Among the Nations. This is an award that Yad Vashem, Israel's Holocaust museum and memorial, gives to non-Jews who helped Jews during the war. It took some time to gather the evidence needed to be able to have them recognized, and in this I received help from Igor Komarovsky, a researcher who did some work for the World-Wide Club of Odessites. Thanks to his wonderful research, Maria and Anna were recognized posthumously by Yad Vashem in August 2009.

Unfortunately, life in retirement doesn't interest me much. I mostly occupy myself with visiting doctors, since illnesses make themselves known with age. My sole outlet is in the meetings of the Song Lovers Club, which was created in Montreal by immigrants from Russia. We meet about once a month, we socialize and, of course, we sing Russian songs. Once a year my husband and I travel to Warsaw to see our daughter and grandson, and the rest of time we lead the life of pensioners, enjoying the simple pleasures of life.

Poem

This poem, written by the well-known Russian poet Valentin Berestov, was dedicated to my father. It was translated by my friend Victor Krupnik.

COMRADE RAKITOV

An open long car loudly honked and stopped by.
It scared away clucking hens and rock pigeons.
A strong man who grabbed me and lifted me high
Was comrade Rakitov, the chief of three regions.

His shirt was as white as he'd dressed for a fest.
That day was too peaceful, the sky was too clear,
And people were coming to welcome the guest.
I sat on his lap and I had no fear.

But long after that I'd recall his white shirt.
The sky had turned black and a fear came later,
And time seemed to stop and my soul was hurt
When he was pronounced a "foe" and a "traitor."

He ran his last meeting and spoke as a chief,
And nobody cared of what he could feel then.
"Whatever will happen, continue to give
Examples of kindness to our children."

Glossary

Ataman (Russian; literally, father-man) The leader of a military force or of a Cossack village.

Bolsheviks (from the Russian word *bol'shinstvo*, majority) A political party in Russia that originated in 1903 after separating from the Russian Social Democratic Labour Party and that came to power during the second half of the 1917 Russian Revolution. The Bolsheviks, founded by Vladimir Lenin and Alexander Bogdanov, were hailed as a proletariat-focused party and eventually became the Communist Party of the Soviet Union. *See also* Communist Party Central Committee, Russian Revolution.

Bund (Yiddish, short for Algemeyner Yidisher Arbeter Bund in Lite, Polyn un Rusland, meaning the Jewish Workers' Alliance in Lithuania, Poland and Russia) A Jewish social-democratic revolutionary movement founded in Vilnius, Lithuania, in 1897 to fight for the rights of the Yiddish-speaking Jewish worker in Eastern Europe, advocate Jewish cultural autonomy in the Diaspora and champion Yiddish language and secular culture.

Canadian Broadcasting Corporation (CBC) The Canadian public service broadcaster. CBC operates a network of English- and French-language radio and television stations across Canada, and also broadcasts in eight Aboriginal languages. In addition, the

CBC operated Radio Canada International, an international service, until 2012. *See also* Radio Canada International.

cheder (Hebrew; literally, room) An Orthodox Jewish elementary school that teaches the fundamentals of Jewish religious observance and textual study, as well as the Hebrew language.

cob wall house A residence constructed with a material made from a mix of soil, straw and water known as cob. Clay or sand is sometimes added for substance. Cob dries to a level of firmness similar to that of concrete.

commissar A Communist Party official assigned to Soviet army units to assure adherence to Party principles and ensure Party loyalty. At different times in the USSR's history, the role of the commissars was very powerful, allowing them to operate outside the military hierarchy and report directly to Party leaders. Political commissars were vital in boosting morale among the troops by reinforcing Communist party ideology and preventing dissension in the ranks.

communal apartment An apartment in the Soviet Union that was shared by several families, with one family to a room. The kitchen, bathroom, hallways and telephone (if there was one) were shared by all the residents. Communal apartments were an attempt to resolve the urban housing crisis that occurred after the Russian Revolution of 1917; due to the government's drive toward industrialization as well as policies of collectivization, people were forced to move from the countryside to the cities for jobs. The existence of the communal apartment did not decline until the 1990s.

Communist Party Central Committee The highest body of the Communist Party of the Soviet Union. Founded by Vladimir Lenin in 1912, the committee set policy for the Bolsheviks and established a group of five members, called a Politburo, to lead the 1917 Russian Revolution. After the Bolsheviks came to power, the committee managed all Communist Party affairs between Party Congresses and functioned as a governing body until the mid–1930s, when most of its membership was executed by Joseph Stalin as he sought to gain control of the Communist Party. After Stalin's death in 1953, the committee continued to function until the dissolution of the Soviet Union in 1991. *See also* Bolsheviks; Politburo; Russian Revolution; Stalin, Joseph.

DXers A term referring to hobbyists who receive and listen to short-wave and other distant radio broadcasts. In telegraphy, DX is a short form for distance transmission.

Ezhov, Nikolai (1895–1940; also Yezhov) The head of the NKVD from 1936 to 1939. During this time, Ezhov coordinated the Stalinist purges of 1934 to 1939, under which many Soviet government and military officials were imprisoned, sent into exile in Siberia, or executed. Many Soviet civilians were also accused of being enemies of the state, with about 1.3 million being arrested and more than 600,000 executed. Ezhov was himself arrested in April 1939 and executed in February 1940. *See also* NKVD.

Gamarnik, Yan (1894–1937; born Jakiv (Yakov) Borysovych Pudykovych) The head of the Political Directorate of the Red Army in 1930. During the time of the Stalinist purges, Garmarnik was accused of engaging in an anti-Soviet conspiracy and committed suicide in 1937.

glasnost (Russian; openness) A policy instituted in the late 1980s by Mikhail Gorbachev, then General Secretary of the Communist Party, to decrease censorship and allow greater freedom of information and transparency in government activities. *See also* Gorbachev, Mikhail.

Gorbachev, Mikhail (1931–) The General Secretary of the Communist Party of the Soviet Union between 1985 and 1991, and president of the Soviet Union from 1990 to 1991. As general secretary, Gorbachev brought in the reform policies of *glasnost* (openness) and *perestroika* (restructuring) in a democratising process that ended the role of the Communist Party in ruling the state. Ultimately, his reforms led to the dissolution of the Soviet Union.

Gorbachev resigned as president in December 1991 after an attempted coup to remove him from power earlier that year.

Kamenev, Lev Borisovich (1883–1936; born Rozenfeld) Soviet-Jewish Bolshevik politician who was a leading member of the Communist Party from 1917 to 1934. During this time, Kamenev was expelled from the Party three times for various oppositional acts, which culminated in his 1934 arrest for alleged conspiracy in the murder of prominent Communist Sergey Kirov. Along with fourteen others, Kamenev was a victim of Stalin's infamous show trials and was executed on August 25, 1936. *See also* Stalin, Joseph; Kirov, Sergey.

Kirov, Sergey Mironovich (1886–1934; born Kostrikov) Head of the Communist Party in Leningrad from 1926 to 1934 and member of the Politburo from 1930. Kirov's increasing popularity among party delegates led to his assassination. There is controversy over whether this was by Stalin's order; nonetheless, Kirov's murder was used as a pretext to begin the Stalinist purges.

Kishinev pogrom An anti-Jewish attack that took place in April 1903 in what was then the capital of Bessarabia in the Russian Empire (now the capital of Moldova). The pogrom was instigated by a local newspaper report of a blood libel – a false accusation that Jews ritually kill Christian children to use their blood in the preparation of matzah for Passover. Over two days, at least 47 Jews were killed and close to 600 were injured, with more than 700 homes destroyed and 600 stores ransacked. It was the first in a series of pogroms against Jews that occurred between 1903 and 1906 in hundreds of cities and small towns across Russia. *See also* pogrom.

Konev, Ivan (1897–1973) A World War II Red Army marshal who helped to push German forces out of much of Eastern Europe and captured Berlin.

Maslenitsa (Russian; cheese-fare week) The week before Lent, a time of fasting and prayer in both Western Christian and Eastern Orthodox traditions. As with Lent, those observing *Maslenitsa* do not eat meat, but can eat both dairy products and eggs, foods that are forbidden during Lent.

Military Revolutionary Committee A military organization created by the Bolshevik Party in 1917 to establish Soviet power in different districts. The Military Revolutionary Committee in Vinnitsa was headed by Nikolai Tarnogrodsky. *See also* Tarnogrodsky, Nikolai.

NKVD (Russian) The acronym of the Narodnyi Komissariat Vnutrennikh Del, meaning People's Commissariat for Internal Affairs. The NKVD functioned as the Soviet Union's security agency, secret police and intelligence agency from 1934 to 1954. The NKVD's Main Directorate for State Security (GUGB) was the forerunner of the Committee for State Security, better known as the KGB (acronym for Komitet Gosudarstvennoy Bezopasnosti) established in 1954. The organization's stated dual purpose was to defend the USSR from external dangers from foreign powers and to protect the Communist Party from perceived dangers within. Under Stalin, the pursuit of imagined conspiracies against the state became a central focus and the NKVD played a critical role in suppressing political dissent. *See also* Stalin, Joseph.

oblast An administrative unit in the former Soviet Union, similar to a state or province.

Ostrovsky, Alexander (1823–1886) A Russian playwright who authored forty-seven plays. His play *Guilty Without Fault* was published in 1883.

Petliura, Symon (1879–1926) A journalist and politician who advocated for an independent Ukraine. Petliura fought against both Bolshevik and White Russian forces in Ukraine and, after World War I, briefly led the Ukrainian government until the country came under Soviet control. In 1924, Petliura settled in Paris, where, two years later, he was assassinated. His legacy is controversial due to the Ukrainian army's pogroms against Jews during his time as leader, when an estimated 35,000 to 50,000 Jews were killed.

pogrom (Russian; to wreak havoc, to demolish) A violent attack on a distinct ethnic group. The term most commonly refers to nineteenth- and twentieth-century attacks on Jews in the Russian Empire. *See also* Kishinev pogrom.

Politburo (in Russian, *politbyuró*; a shortened form of *politícheskoe byuró*, political bureau) The executive committee of the Communist Party Central Committee, originally created to oversee the Bolshevik Revolution in October 1917. The Politburo quickly became the dominant state policy-making forum and governing body, with the position of First or General Secretary wielding the greatest power, most notably under the leadership of Joseph Stalin (1924–1953). When the Soviet Union was dissolved in 1991 and the Communist Party was banned, the Politburo was dissolved as well. *See also* Communist Party Central Committee; Stalin, Joseph.

Pushkin, Alexander (1799–1837) A Russian poet and novelist, considered the father of modern Russian literature.

Radio Canada International (RCI) An international shortwave and satellite radio broadcasting service offered by the Canadian Broadcasting Corporation. Initiated in the 1940s, it broadcast in fourteen languages until June 2012, when budget cuts resulted in its termination as a shortwave and satellite service. RCI continues to be available on the internet in five languages.

Red Army (in Russian, *Krasnaya Armiya*) A term used from 1918 to 1946 for the Soviet Union's armed forces, which were founded when the Bolshevik Party came to power after the Russian Revolution. The original name was the Workers' and Peasants' Red Army, the colour red representing blood spilled while struggling against oppression.

Rumyantsev, Ivan Petrovich (1885–1937) The first secretary of the Communist Party's *oblast* committee in Smolensk from January 1929 to June 1937. He was arrested in 1937 and executed during Stalin's purges.

Russian Revolution The 1917 February and October revolutions that led to the dissolution of the autocratic tsarist regime and the creation of a Communist government, respectively. The provisional government established after the February revolt was defeated by the Bolsheviks in October. The Bolshevik government – also referred to as the "reds" – was subsequently challenged by the "whites" or anti-Bolsheviks, which resulted in a five-year civil war. *See also* Bolsheviks, Communist Party Central Committee.

samovar (Russian; literally, self-boil) A metal urn under which a small fire is lit to keep water hot. A concentrated brew of tea is kept in a teapot on top of the urn and diluted with water from the samovar for drinking.

Shelekhes, Ilya Savelyevich (1891–1938) The chairman of the Communist Party's executive committee for the Smolensk *oblast* from January 1929 to February 1933 and the Kharkiv *oblast* from 1933 to 1934. Shelekhes was murdered during the Stalinist purges.

Siguranța Statului (Romanian; State Security) The Romanian secret police, which was established in 1908. The Siguranța was dissolved in 1948 and amalgamated into Romania's Department of State Security or *Securitate*.

Smolensk Archive A large collection of the records of the Smolensk *oblast* committee of the Communist Party of the Soviet Union, covering a time frame from about 1917 to 1941 and comprising over 200,000 pages of documents. The archive includes minutes of city and district committee meetings and decisions; information about policies affecting agriculture, trade unions, industry and the military; letters of complaint from Soviet citizens; and files of the secret police and Communist Party purges. The archive was seized by the Nazis in 1941 and first taken to Germany, then to Poland. In 1945, American troops found the archive; the US held the inventory for use by Western scholars until 2002, when it returned all materials to Russia.

Snegov, Alexei Vladimirovich (1898–1989) The secretary of the municipal committee of the Vinnitsa underground in 1918. Snegov went on to hold various positions on Communist Party provincial and district committees in Podolsky, Zinoviev and Ukraine. Though arrested in June 1937 as part of the Stalinist purges, Snegov was acquitted and released in January 1939, only to be arrested again and held as a political prisoner until 1954.

Stalin, Joseph (1878–1953) The leader of the Soviet Union from 1924 until his death in 1953. Born Joseph Vissarionovich Dzhugashvili, he changed his name to Stalin (literally: man of steel) in 1903. He was a staunch supporter of Lenin, taking control of the Communist Party upon Lenin's death. Very soon after acquiring leadership of the Communist Party, Stalin ousted rivals, killed opponents in purges, and effectively established himself as a dictator. During the late 1930s, Stalin commenced "The Great Purge," during which he targeted and disposed of elements within the Communist Party that he deemed to be a threat to the stability of the Soviet Union. These purges extended to both military and civilian society, and millions of people were incarcerated or exiled to harsh labour camps. After World War II, Stalin set up Communist governments controlled by Moscow in many Eastern European states bordering and close to the USSR, and instituted antisemitic campaigns and purges.

Star of David (in Hebrew, *Magen David*) The six-pointed star that is the ancient and most recognizable symbol of Judaism. During World War II, Jews in Nazi-occupied areas were frequently forced to wear a badge or armband with the Star of David on it as an identifying mark of their lesser status and to single them out as targets for persecution.

Tarnogrodsky, Nikolai Pavlovich (1894–1938) The chairman of the Revolutionary Committee of Vinnitsa during the Russian Revolution. In the 1920s he worked for the Communist Party in the Urals, North Caucasus and Far East. Tarnogrodsky was executed during the Stalinist purges of the late 1930s.

Timoshenko, Semyon (1895–1970) A commander in the Red Army during the 1930s and World War II, Timoshenko became the Commissar for Defence and Marshal of the Soviet Union in 1940 and fought on the central front near Smolensk.

Transnistria A 16,000-square-mile region between the Dniester and Bug rivers that originally had been part of Ukraine. After German and Romanian forces conquered Ukraine in the summer of 1941, Romania administered this territory and deported hundreds of thousands of Jews there, where many were killed or died of illness and starvation.

Tukhachevsky, Mikhail Nikolayevich (1893–1937) A Soviet military leader who helped to modernize and reshape the Soviet army's structure and weaponry. Tukhachevsky served as chief of staff of the Red Army from 1925 to 1928 and commander of the Leningrad Military District from 1928 to 1931 before becoming deputy head of the Military Council in 1931. He was accused of treason and executed in 1937 during Stalin's Great Purge.

Uborevich, Yeronim (1896–1937; also Ieronim; Lithuanian: Jeronimas Uborevičius) A Lithuanian-born military leader who joined the Bolshevik Party in March 1917 and held command posts in the Red Army during the Russian civil war. Uborevich served as War Minister in the Far Eastern Republic, a state that existed briefly between Russia and Japan, and commanded two military districts until 1937, when he was arrested during the Stalinist purges and executed.

White Army The armed forces of the White Russians who fought the Soviet Red Army and Bolshevism during the 1917–1920 Russian civil war.

Yad Vashem The Holocaust Martyrs' and Heroes' Remembrance Authority, established in 1953 to commemorate, educate the public about, research and document the Holocaust.

Yakir, Yona Emmanuilovich (1896–1937; also Iona Iakir) A decorated Red Army commander who was murdered during Stalin's Great Purge in 1937. Yakir joined the Bolshevik Party in 1917 and commanded various military divisions before serving as Commander of the Ukrainian Military District from 1925 to 1935 and of the Third Red Army Formation from 1935 to 1937. In May 1937 he was arrested and accused, along with Tukhachevsky, Uborevich and others, of being Nazi agents and members of an anti-Soviet military organization.

Zakovsky, Leonid Mihajlovich (1894–1938; born Henriks Ernestovich Stubis) The head of the NKVD in Leningrad. Initially a member of Cheka (All-Russian Extraordinary Commission to Combat Counterrevolution and Sabotage) and head of the State Political Directorate in Siberia, Zakovsky was elected to the Supreme Soviet of the USSR in December 1937. In January 1938 he became head of the NKVD for Moscow. Zakovsky was arrested in April 1938 and executed four months later. *See also* NKVD.

Zhukov, Georgy (1896–1974) A Soviet Red Army commander and marshal of the Soviet Union who led the defense of both Moscow and Stalingrad during World War II, and lifted the siege of Leningrad (St. Petersburg) on January 27, 1944. Zhukov, credited with liberating the Soviet Union and eastern Poland, also led offensives in Belorussia as well as the final battle leading to the surrender of Berlin in April 1945.

Photographs

The Brik family. Standing in the back row, left to right: Maya's uncle Adam and aunt Sonya; Maya's youngest uncle, Sasha; Maya's aunt Nina; and her uncles Ber and Senya. Middle row, left to right: an unidentified woman; Aunt Betya; Maya's grandparents Moses and Sima holding their twin grandsons, Vova and Jenya; and Uncle Arkady. Seated in front: Maya's cousin Judith; Maya's brother, Leonid; and Maya's cousin Miriam. Vinnitsa, summer 1931.

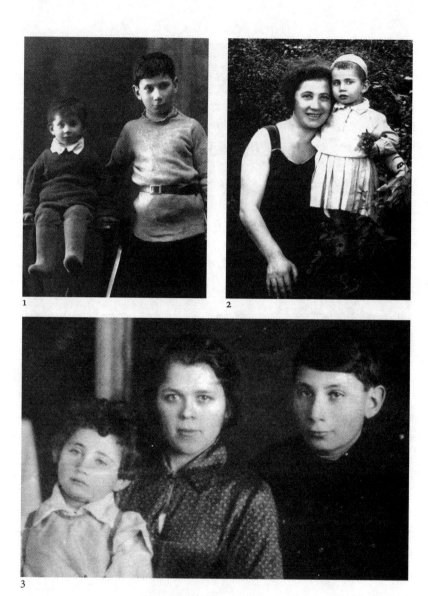

1 Maya, age 2, and her brother, Leonid. Smolensk, 1933.
2 Maya with her mother, Zinaida, outside the cottage near Smolensk. Summer 1934.
3 Maya (left), her nanny, Nyura (centre), and her brother, Leonid. Smolensk, 1935.

Maya's father, Grigory Davidovich Rakitov. 1930s.

В ЭТОМ ДОМЕ
в 1930-1935 гг.
ЖИЛ ЧЛЕН КПСС
с 1913 года,
АКТИВНЫЙ УЧАСТНИК
ГРАЖДАНСКОЙ ВОЙНЫ,
ПРЕДСЕДАТЕЛЬ ИСПОЛКОМА
ЗАПАДНОЙ ОБЛАСТИ
ГРИГОРИЙ ДАВЫДОВИЧ
РАКИТОВ

Memorial plaque in honour of Maya's father, which was placed on the house in Smolensk where the Rakitovs lived until 1935.

1   Maya's mother, Zinaida. Leningrad, 1950s.
2   Passport photo of Zinaida. 1960s.

Maya's brother, Leonid. 1960s.

Maya Rakitova. Montreal, 2005.

Index

"Account of a Life Story Fact-
Finding" (Komarovsky), xxiv

Adya (Sonya Brik's husband), 26,
27, 30

Ajzensztadt, Amnon, xxii

Alexianu, Gheorghe, xxi

Andrievsky, Piotr (friend of Moisie
Brik), 30

Antonescu, Ion, xxi

Ataman (leader of military force), 4

Babi Yar (Kiev), xxi

Berestov, Valentin, 55

Berkhoff, Karel C., xxiii

*Bloodlands: Europe Between Hitler
and Stalin* (Snyder), xv

Bolshevik Party (Russian Social
Democratic Labour Party), 4

Bolsheviks, xvi, xvii, 1, 3, 4, 9, 10.

Brichany/Briceni (Moldova), xvi,
3, 4

Brik, Arkady (maternal uncle), 6,
19, 45

Brik, Betya (maternal aunt), 19, 45

Brik, Boris (maternal uncle), 21–22,
25, 28, 45

Brik, Moisie (Moshe; maternal
grandfather), 1–2, 21–23, 27, 28,
29–30, 33

Brik, Nina (maternal aunt), 19

Brik, Senya (maternal uncle), 45

Brik, Sima (maternal grandmother), 1, 21, 29

Brik, Sonya (maternal aunt), 15–16,
25–29

Brik, Zinaida (mother): birth, 1;
childhood, 2; courtship/mar-
riage, 2–3, 5–7; spirit, 6–7,
11–12, 13; life in Smolensk, 11–12;
evading Stalin's prison camps,
18–23; surviving Nazi-occupied
Ukraine, 25–35, 38–39, 40, 43;
courage, 6, 15, 27, 30–31, 32, 33,
35, 43; return to Vinnitsa, 45–47;
in Chernivtsi and Leningrad, 48,
49, 50; death, 50

Bund (General Jewish Workers'
Union), 4

CBC (Canadian Broadcasting

Corporation), 51

Cheka (Soviet political police), xvi

Chernivtsi (Romania/Ukraine), 47

Civil War (Russia), xvii, 4, 5, 10–11, 12

commissars (political leaders), 5, 10

communal apartments, 11

Communist Party Central Committee, xvii, 4, 5

"Comrade Rakitov" (Berestov), 55

Donskoy Cemetery (Moscow), 18

Dumitru, Diana, xxiii

DXers (shortwave radio enthusiasts), 52

Einsatzgruppe C, xx

Einsatzgruppen (killing squads), xix

Einsatzkommando 6, xx

Ezhov, Nikolai, 16

Fainsod, Merle, xviii

Family Members of Traitors of the Motherland law, xviii, 16, 18

45th Rifle Division (Odessa), 5, 6, 10

Gamarnik, Yan, 10–11

German Reserve Police Battalion 45, xx

Germany: invasion of Ukraine, xx, 25–30; occupation of Ukraine, xviii–xx, 27–34; in retreat from Odessa, 43–45

Gerstenfeld-Maltiel, Jacob, xxii

Gorbachev, Mikhail, 17

GPU (Soviet political police), xvi

Great Terror, xviii, xxii, xxx, 3, 5–6, 9, 10, 11, 16–17

Guilty Without Fault (Ostrovsky), 48

Harvest of Despair: Life and Death in Ukraine under Nazi Rule (Berkhoff), xxiii

Hitler, Adolf, xx, 27

Holocaust, Ukraine, xviii–xx, xxx, 25–30

Holocaust and Modernity (journal), xv

Irina (daughter), 49, 50

"Jewish Bolshevism," xvi

Jews: in Soviet Union, xvi–xvii; in Transnistria, xxi–xxii; in Holocaust in Ukraine, xviii–xx, xxx, 25–30

Kaluga (Ukraine), 7, 9

Kamenev, Lev, xvii, 9

Kazatin (Koziatyn; Ukraine), 33–34

Khomichuk, Maria, 29, 30, 32, 52

Kirichenko, Irina (friend), 22

Kirichenko, Mrs. (teacher), 22

Kirov, Sergey, 5

Kishinev/Chişinău (Russia/Moldova), xvii, 3, 4

Koch, Erich (Reichskommissar), xviii. See also Holocaust, Ukraine

Komarovsky, Igor, xxii, xxiv

Konev, Ivan, 16

Kruglov, Alexander, xix, xx

Krupnik, Victor, xxvii, 55

Ladispoli (Italy), 51

Lazarev (father's bodyguard), 15, 16

Leningrad, 48–49

Lerner, Alexander (Judith's husband), 26

Lerner, Inga, 26, 28–29

Lerner, Judith (Ditha; maternal cousin), 26

Lerner, Vita, 26, 28–29

Linda (friend of Anna Mikheyeva), 35, 39

Lopatov (driver), 14

Lubyanka prison (Moscow), 17

Lucjan (husband), 49–50, 51

Marfusha (Ilya Vainer's saviour), 32

Maslenitsa (cheese-fare week), 34

McGill University (Montreal), 51

Mikheyeva, Anna (Anastasia), xv, xxii, 34–42, 52

Military Revolutionary Committee, 4

Miriam (Mira; maternal cousin), 26

Nadya (friend in Odessa), 44–45

NKVD (People's Commissariat for Internal Affairs), xvi, xviii, 5–6, 16, 18

Nyura (nanny), 11–12, 16

Nyusya, 28, 29

oblasts (provinces), xvii, 9, 15

Odessa (Transnistria), xviii, xxi, 4–5, 10, 19–21, 35–45

Oknitsky/Ocniţa (Moldova), 3

Old Town (Vinnitsa), 1, 22, 27, 29–31, 45, 47. *See also* Vinnitsa/Vinnytsia (Ukraine)

Olga (mother's friend), 30, 32, 33

Ostrovsky, Alexander, 48

Palace of Pioneers (Chernivtsi), 47–48

Palace of Young Pioneers (Odessa), 45

Paulina (daughter), 50, 51

Petliura, Symon, xvii, 4, 6

Philipovna, Theophilia, 37–38

Podolia region (Ukraine), xviii, xix, 6

Pogrebishche (Ukraine), 33

pogroms, xvii, 3, 4

Poland, xv, xxi, 4, 39, 40, 49, 50, 51, 52

Poltava (Ukraine), 7

Pretzel, Marian, xxii

Pushkin, Alexander, 14

Rabinovich, Doctor (paternal uncle), 19

Rabinovich, Grigory (father). *See* Rakitov, Grigory (father)

Radio and Television Project Bureau (Warsaw), 50

Radio Canada International (RCI), xxx, 51–52

Rakitov, Alik (Leonid's son), 46

Rakitov, Grigory (father): birth, xvi, 2; early years, 3–4; courtship/marriage, 2–3, 5–7; as revolutionist, xvii, 3–7; reason for name change, xvii; Communist Party committee work, xvii–xviii, 6, 9–11, 15–17; principles, 10–11, 13–14; in Smolensk, 9–11; in Kursk, 15–17; arrest and execution, xviii, 15–18; poetry tribute, 55

Rakitov, Leonid (brother): birth, 7; memories, 9–10, 13–14, 17–18; escape from Vinnitsa, 26; war experiences, 46, 48; career, 11, 48; death, xxvii

Rakitova, Maya: birth, xvi; youth in
    Vinnitsa and Odessa, 18–23; in
    Nazi-occupied Vinnitsa, 25–32;
    in wartime Transnistria, 34–36;
    in wartime Odessa, 37–45; as
    Maria, xxi, 32–33; in post-war
    Ukraine, 45–48; education, 22,
    23, 41, 46, 47–49; marriage and
    children, 49–50; career, 50, 51–
    52; in Canada, 51–52; perspective
    on the past, xxiii, xxx; sources
    for information on parents, 5, 6,
    7, 9–10, 13–14, 17
Red Army, 4, 5, 6, 10–11, 12, 16, 45
Reich Labour Service, xix
Reichskommissariat Ukraine, xviii
Righteous Among the Nations, xv,
    xxii, 52
Rumyantsev, Ivan, 9, 15, 18
Russian Civil War, xvii, 4, 5, 10–11,
    12
Shelekhes, Ilya, 9–10
Shoah Visual History Foundation,
    xv
Siguranța (Romanian secret police),
    37, 40, 41
Smolensk (Russian Soviet Federal
    Socialist Republic), xvi, xvii, 9
Smolensk Archive, xvii–xviii, 13
Smolensk under Soviet Rule
    (Fainsod), xviii
Snegov, Alexei, 4
Snyder, Timothy, xv
Song Lovers Club (Montreal), 52
Soviet political police, xvi
Soviet Union. See also Stalin,
    Joseph; under communism, xvii,
    10–11; German invasion of, 25–
    30; liberation of Odessa, 43–45;
    policy toward Jews, xvi–xvii
Spielberg, Steven, xv
Stalin, Joseph: policy toward Jews,
    xvi–xvii; Great Terror, xviii, xxii,
    xxix, 3, 5–6, 9, 10, 11, 16–17; and
    Grigory Rakitov, xviii, 9, 16, 17,
    21; purges, 5, 11, 16–17; law re-
    garding family of traitors, xviii,
    16, 18; death, xv, xxii, 49
Star of David, xx, 27
Tarnogrodsky, Nikolai, 4
"The Holocaust in Ukraine"
    (Berkhoff), xxiii
"The Last Jew," xix
The State, Antisemitism, and
    Collaboration in the Holocaust:
    The Borderlands of Romania and
    the Soviet Union (Dumitru),
    xxiii
"The Two Victories of My Mother"
    (Rakitova), xv
"The Untold Stories: The Murder
    Sites of the Jews in the Occupied
    Territories of the Former USSR"
    (Yad Vashem), xxiv
Timoshenko, Semyon, 12
Transnistria (Ukraine), xviii,
    xx–xxi, 34–36. See also Odessa
    (Transnistria)
Tukhachevsky, Mikhail, 11, 16
Uborevich, Yeronim, xvii, 11, 12–13,
    16, 18
Ukraine: German invasion of, xx,

25–30; under German occupa-
tion, xviii–xx, 27–34; Holocaust,
xviii–xx, xxx, 25–30; Jewish
citizens in, xvi, xvii
United States Holocaust Memorial
Museum, xix
Vainer, Dina (Leonid Rakitov's
wife), 26, 31, 46
Vainer, Ilya (Dina's father), 31–32
Vapniarka (Transnistria), 34–36
Vinnitsa/Vinnytsia (Ukraine):
description, 1–3; during civil
war, 4–6, 16, 18–19; under Nazi
occupation, xviii–xx, xxx, 25–30;
liberation, 45–46
Vinokurova, Faina, xx
Volshonok, Jacob, 17
Waffen-SS, xix
Warsaw (Poland), 52
Western Oblast (region), 9
White Army, 4, 5, 6, 10–11
World-Wide Club of Odessites,
xxii, 52
Yad Vashem, xv, xxiv, 52
Yakir, Yona, xvii, 4, 5, 6, 16
Yerusalimka district (Vinnitsa), 1
Yiddish, xvi, xvii, xx, 22
Zakovsky, Leonid, xviii, 5–6, 18
Zhukov, Georgy, 16

The Azrieli Foundation was established in 1989 to realize and extend the philanthropic vision of David J. Azrieli, C.M., C.Q., M.Arch. The Foundation's mission is to support a wide spectrum of initiatives in education and research. The Azrieli Foundation is an active supporter of programs in the fields of Education, the education of architects, scientific and medical research, and the arts. The Azrieli Foundation's many initiatives include: the Holocaust Survivor Memoirs Program, which collects, preserves, publishes and distributes the written memoirs of survivors in Canada; the Azrieli Institute for Educational Empowerment, an innovative program successfully working to keep at-risk youth in school; the Azrieli Fellows Program, which promotes academic excellence and leadership on the graduate level at Israeli universities; the Azrieli Music Project, which celebrates and fosters the creation of high-quality new Jewish orchestral music; and the Azrieli Neurodevelopmental Research Program, which supports advanced research on neurodevelopmental disorders, particularly Fragile X and Autism Spectrum Disorders.